GRADED LESSONS IN

Macramé, Knotting
and Netting

GRADED LESSONS IN

Macramé, Knotting and Netting

*(former title:
Varied Occupations in String Work)*

BY

LOUISA
WALKER

DOVER PUBLICATIONS, INC.
NEW YORK

Published in Canada by General Publishing Company, Ltd., 30 Lesmill Road, Don Mills, Toronto, Ontario.

Published in the United Kingdom by Constable and Company, Ltd., 10 Orange Street, London WC 2.

This Dover edition, first published in 1971, is an unabridged and unaltered republication of the work originally published by Macmillan and Co., Ltd., London, in 1896 with the title *Varied Occupations in String Work: Comprising Knotting, Netting, Looping, Plaiting, and Macramé.*

International Standard Book Number: 0-486-22754-5
Library of Congress Catalog Card Number: 73-158734

Manufactured in the United States of America
Dover Publications, Inc.
180 Varick Street
New York, N. Y. 10014

PREFACE

Section I. treats of tying knots and making cords in the hands only, without the aid of the desk. Section II. consists of knots and cords tied or built up upon a foundation. Section III. treats of knots and cords made in Sections I. and II. with Macramé knotting so manipulated as to form laces and geometrical designs. The number of uses to which the work can be applied, together with its infinite variety and durability, make it an occupation desirable for children.

LOUISA WALKER.

Fleet Road Board School,
Hampstead, 1895.

CONTENTS

STAGE I.

STAGE II.

STAGE III.

ILLUSTRATIONS.

STAGE I.

GRADED LESSONS IN

Macramé, Knotting and Netting

NOTE : The suppliers and prices of materials mentioned in this book are naturally no longer valid, but the reader will easily be able to find local suppliers or improvise substitute materials.

STAGE I.

SIMPLE KNOTTING AND CORDS.

THIS Stage is suitable for children of five and six years of age, who require training in using their fingers. The educational aim will be to teach colour and the blending of the same, deftness of touch, and the power of numbers up to four.

All the exercises can be worked and held in the hands, so that the occupation can be taught in a class without the need of desks.

Each lesson should be demonstrated with large coloured cords before the children, and those that are sharp and learn quickly should be set to teach others, for many a little child will better understand the difficulty of its neighbour than the teacher.

The work progresses rapidly, and the difficulties that repel many at first sight are only on the surface. Any teacher who carefully follows the instructions given in this little volume will soon overcome them, and be able without much trouble to teach any number of children by simple demonstration. "Do as I do," and "then as I say," should be the teacher's mode of procedure. Too much stress cannot be laid upon this point, for upon the demonstration of the teacher the ultimate results will depend. A child will readily understand what it can follow with its eyes, when it might fail to understand from verbal explanation.

To meet the requirements of children of all ages in infant schools the occupation is graded into three Stages, viz. : Stage I. treats of knots made on the fingers only. Stage II. treats of knots of greater difficulty, which require a foundation and the use of more than two strings. Stage III. consists of the combination of knots taught in Stages I. and II. manipulated into geometrical designs for laces.

Materials required.—The materials are simple and inexpensive, and if a few large reels or ribbon rollers with centre holes be provided for the cords, every exercise in this Stage can be worked by an average infant.

Note.—The ribbon rollers may be obtained gratuitously from any draper, and those used for ribbon velvet have a drilled hole which exactly answers the purpose.

String.—The string must be soft and pliable, and the macramé string of the coarse make is most suitable for beginners. A coarser kind of cord is manufactured specially for the teacher's use, which should be used for demonstration purposes. Let the turn of every new knot be clearly understood before allowing the children to work on their own strings. This can easily be ascertained by calling upon individual children to work before the class. The work must be done tightly and evenly, and each knot drawn in its place before the next is worked.

WHY KNOTTING IS SUITABLE FOR CHILDREN.

1. It can be taught simultaneously to large classes by demonstration and from blackboard illustration.

2. It is a fascinating and pleasant occupation.

3. It is durable and useful.

4. It is easily and quickly learned and executed.

5. It makes both hands work equally.

6. It makes a child attentive and thoughtful.

7. It appeals to the inventive and designing faculties.

8. It strengthens the muscles of the arms.

9. It teaches geometrical terms, horizontal, vertical, oblique, etc.

10. It can be easily undone and the string used again.

11. It is an occupation which can be continued in the upper schools, made in finer threads, silks, etc.

12. It teaches colour (balls of string of various shades), and number.

Uses of knotting.—It is often necessary to join two threads or strings together, which is done by means of knots. Knots, or what may resemble them, are employed in making designs for fringes and other decorative work. There are knots which, when made with thick braid or cord, are useful for trimming dresses and jackets. The basis of all macramé is knots which are made by the fingers, tying tightly together short ends of string, either in horizontal, oblique, or vertical lines, and interweaving the knots so made to form a design. From the nature of the work the patterns thus made are simple and geometrical in form. Macramé is celebrated for its durability and excellence. The coarser kind made of string is used for mantel-borders, and other furniture trimmings. The finer kind in silk and thread can be used as edgings for garments and fringes of vestments, altar cloths, etc.

EXERCISES.

I. COMMON KNOT. TO TIE A SINGLE KNOT.

Age of Children.—Five years.

Aim of Lesson.—

    1. To teach colour and number.

    2. To teach distance and measurement.

    3. To give deftness to the fingers.

Materials required.—1. A yard of string for each child.

    2. A yard of coarse string for teacher's use.

Lesson.—The teacher should stand in front of class in such a position that the children can see every step of the process and follow her movements, thus—

    1. *Show strings.*—The children to show the strings by holding one end in either hand.

    2. *Double strings in half.*—Bring the two ends together and hold in left hand.

    3. *Show doubled strings.*—Put the first finger of right hand in the loop which is hanging down, and hold the loop between the first finger and thumb of right hand in a horizontal position. The strings are now half a yard in length, and opportunity should be taken at this point to teach the divisions of a yard into halves and quarters. It will give the children some idea of the different measurements if they actually hold out their strings and divide them into the halves and quarters. The teacher might

interest the children by telling them how the first yard measure was obtained, that a certain king named Henry had his arm measured, and called the length of it one yard. He also had his foot measured, and this was twelve inches long, and three times the measurement of his foot was as long as his arm. Let the children now divide their strings into three and repeat "Three feet make one yard." At this stage the colour of the strings should be spoken of and compared to flowers and other objects of similar colour known to the children.

4. *Tie a single knot at the half.*—Hold the middle of string in the left hand and pass one end round the first finger to form a loop, and then pass the end through the loop which is formed on the finger and pull tight. This constitutes a single knot called "The overhand knot," and is used for making a knot in a cord where it requires shortening, or to connect two ends together. Hold the knot made in left hand, and pass string round finger as before and make a second knot. Pull tightly with right hand, but keep hold of the knot until the next is finished. Proceed making knots in this way till one half yard is used up, then turn the string and again hold centre knot and proceed to knot the other half in similar manner. By starting from the half it is found easier for the children because they have less string each time to pull through the loop, and tangles are thus avoided. Regularity in the distance apart of the knots is also obtained.

II. LETTER LAYING WITH KNOTTED STRINGS.

Uses.—This kind of knot is used largely for finishing off the ends of macramé lace, and will be found very useful for that work. When the strings are fully knotted the children might lay them in various designs upon their slates or desks, or they might be wetted and then shaped into *letters* to train the inventive faculties of the children.

FIG. 1.

The knotted strings look well if sewn over traced patterns, either upon paper or material, and form an occupation for children in Stages II. and III., where the strings might be utilized to form a decoration for mats, tidies, wall-texts, mottoes, etc. Children are delighted when they see their efforts are worthy of praise from their teacher, and their work can be utilized to some good purpose. It is, therefore, desirable that the teacher should have some definite object in view for which to encourage the children. The articles in Ex. III. to Ex. V. are suitable for using up the strings.

III.   A BOY'S WHIP OF SINGLE KNOTTED STRINGS.

A round blind-stick which will cost a halfpenny is sufficient for three handles of whips. Those children who produce regular knotted strings might be allowed to make a whip.

The thong.—Take several lengths of the knotted strings and plait in three for about 6 inches. Wind the ends round with thread very tightly and cut off even, then attach to the handle.

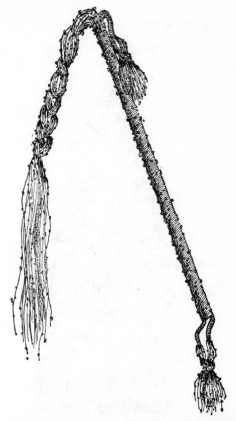

Fig. 2.

The handle.—Place the thong flatly and evenly round the end of the stick, and with *unknotted* string wind closely round the stick till the thong is covered. Let a child finish winding the remainder of stick with knotted string, and secure the end by sewing with needle and

thread, or a small tack.　The whip looks better if ornamented with a tassel or two.

IV. A TASSEL OF SINGLE KNOTTED STRINGS.

The tassels are easily made by cutting the knotted
strings into lengths of 10 inches, then tying several to-

Fig. 3.

gether tightly at the half with an unknotted string.　Let
the ends fall down, and hold these together in the left
hand, whilst the doubled top is overwound with string.
The top of the tassel might be much improved by a
simple chain of crochet round the top as in the illustra-

tion. The tassels look well attached to the top of the whip where the thong is joined, and also at the handle.

Knotted fringe.—Very useful fringe for trimming the childrens' basket-work or for brackets may also be made from these knotted strings. Cut the strings into lengths of 6 or 8 inches, and double each length in half. Place the loop end at top, and with bone crochet-hook and ball of macramé string of the same colour as the knotted lengths, proceed to crochet a simple chain, and before taking each stitch place across a knotted string, or fold the loop end in the left hand and draw the chain through the two loops at the same time.

V. A WORK-TABLE, TRIMMED WITH KNOTTED FRINGE.

The little bamboo work-basket in the illustration is one of those sold by any fancy draper at 4¾d. It is trimmed and ornamented with knotted fringe and tassels like those described. The three legs are overwound like the handle of a whip, with a continuous length of unknotted string. They are tied together and ornamented with three tassels at the jointure, whilst at the top of each leg are added two more tassels. The inside of the basket may (if desired) be lined, but if it is, the lining should be frilled round and be quite in harmony with the colour of the string. These tripod baskets are easily made by the boys in the cane-weaving class. A round shallow basket of 18 inches diameter is needed for the top, and three bamboo canes crossed and tied as in illustration on next page will complete the tripod (see Fig. 4).

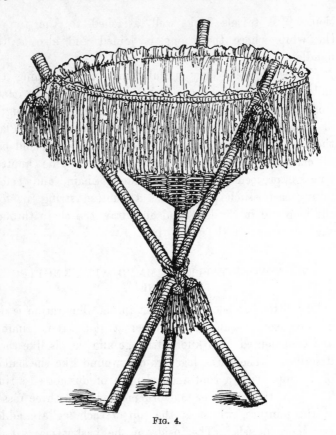

FIG. 4.

VI. A SINGLE TIE KNOT OF TWO STRINGS. (SEE FIG. 5.)

It is often necessary to join strings together, and this is
the most simple and common form of joining.   The method
employed is exactly the same as that in Ex. I., except
that two strings are knotted each time instead of one.

1. Take the ends of both strings in either hand and
hold out horizontally.

2. Double in half, bringing all four ends together.
Find the half.

3. Hold both strings at the half and pass round the

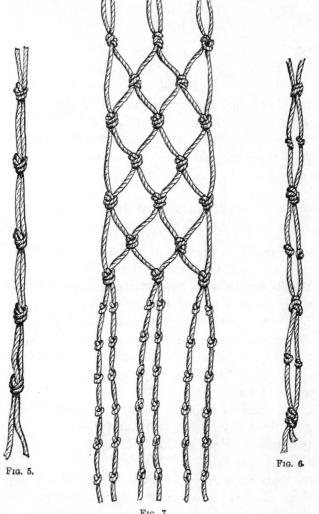

Fig. 5.   Fig. 6.

Fig. 7.

fingers, and knot as before till both ends are used up.
Keep the knots at equal distances apart.

VII. SINGLE AND DOUBLE STRINGS KNOTTED WITH A SINGLE KNOT. (See Fig. 6.)

This exercise is a combination of Ex. I. and Ex. VI. Give each child two strings of equal length of either the same or different colours, and knot them together (Ex. VI.) Then holding the double knot in the left hand make a single knot on each string separately.

The two single knots are now held together, and a knot of the double strings repeated. The exercise continues in this way until the string is used up.

VIII. A KNOTTED FRINGE OF SINGLE AND DOUBLE STRINGS. (See Fig. 7.)

Any number of strings may be joined together according to Ex. VII. and make an effective fringe. To do this, all the strings must be knotted together in turn. For a first exercise give the children two colours so that they readily know which strings to take each time. In the illustration red and white strings are used alternately.

Row 1. Take a white string and knot to the next red one, and place them in position upon the desk (Ex. VI.) in sets or pairs.

Row 2. Take the right-hand string of one set (red) and knot to the left string of the next (white).

Row 3 is the same as the first.

Row 4 is the same as the second.

The ends are knotted in single knots (Ex. I.).

Older children could carry this exercise to a much greater extent and make long curtains, hammocks, and lawn-tennis nets. It has much the appearance of netting.

IX. A KNOTTED SHOPPING OR HAND BAG.

Materials required.—1. Brown macramé string, cut into lengths of one yard and a half.

2. Small steel or brass curtain-rings the size of a farthing.

Lesson.—Distribute to each child a ring and three strings. Double each string in half. Pass the ends up through the ring, and bring them over the rim and down

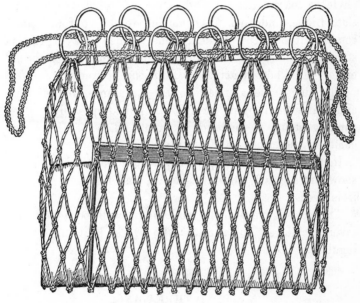

FIG. 8.

through the loop. This is called "Casting on," and will be needed throughout all the exercises.

Knot the three strings on the ring in this way, and let the children tie every pair once as described in Ex. VI. Collect.

As the whole of the bag has to be in one piece, and all adjoining strings knotted together, the bag can only be finished by one or two children

Thread the rings upon a stick, and see that the casting on side is the same throughout; let a child knot the whole according to the method of Ex. VIII. The teacher must start him right for each row, because the end strings will have to be knotted together every alternate row to close the bag together. The rings could be threaded upon a circle of coarse wire, or tied round any object such as a slate frame, and then the knotting would go round and round without any interruption. When the depth is sufficient the piece is folded in half, and the ends of either half knotted across to form the bottom.

The rings give a much better appearance to the bag, and enable the running string to be pulled up easily. The running string is made of a simple chain of the same colour as described in Ex. XVIII.

In the illustration a parcel is placed inside the bag to show more clearly how it is made, and for what purpose it is used.

The cost is very little, and might well be taken by several children in a class who work Ex. VIII. with regularity.

BEAD AND STRING WORK.

X.   BEAD THREADING.

Bead-threading is always a fascinating employment for young children, because it is not only pleasing and interesting to the child, but affords a valuable means of instruction. Bead threading teaches colour, number, awakens the child's intelligence, and forms a desirable manual training for little fingers. The early lessons are begun in the babies' room, and are most valuable in training the hands to become steady for needle threading.

Beads.—The beads used are large and of various colours. Those generally used for school purposes are round, smooth, glass beads; black, white, red, blue, yellow, and green in colour.

Saucers.—Each child is provided with a small tin saucer or wooden bowl in which to hold the beads, and these can be bought at sixpence the dozen. The wooden saucers have an advantage over the tin ones, because they are, comparatively speaking, noiseless.

Strings.—The ordinary shop twine is suitable for the threading, but it needs waxing to keep the ends from fraying. Coarse carpet thread would answer the same purpose.

The Lesson.—Materials required.—1. Give to each child a saucer, twelve beads of two different colours (white and black), and a string 12 inches long. It is best to tie a bead on the end of each string before the lesson. At the command of the teacher the children should work with her thus :

Take strings in right hand and rub the end between the first finger and thumb of the left hand, to make it smooth and pointed.

2. Take a white bead in left hand. Thread.

3. Take a black bead in left hand. Thread. The children repeat: "One white bead" and "one black bead." Question how many beads are threaded. Introduce simple stories and liken the beads to living animals, as two little birds in a nest, or a dog and a cat in the same house, and relate some anecdote to arouse the children's intelligence. Remember to let the children speak in short sentences whenever possible, because this is the time for increasing their vocabulary. The children might learn a

song about the clock, and use their string of beads as a pendulum. Every new exercise would be treated more or less in the same way.

The exercises in order of difficulty are:

1. One black bead and one white bead. (Two.)
2. One black bead and one white bead, and one red bead. (Three.)
3. Two white beads and one blue bead. (Three.)
4. Two blue beads and two yellow beads. (Four.)
5. Three red beads and one green bead. (Four.)
6. Three yellow beads and two blue beads. (Five.)
7. Three black beads and three red beads. (Six.)
8. Two red, two green, two yellow. (Six.)
9. Three white, two red, two blue. (Seven.)
10. Three green, three red, three black. (Nine.)

The exercises may be further extended and be made the stepping-stone to the addition and subtraction of numbers. In the hands of a skilful teacher, bead threading might be made one of the most interesting educative occupations taught. At the end of each lesson, the children should carefully slip off the beads into their saucers, and then pick out all of one colour, and put into teacher's box as she collects; this should be done for each separate colour, and it will be a good exercise for the child.

XI. FLY REST.

Another very pretty way of using the large glass beads is by introducing coloured straws and silks, and making "Fly Rests" (see Fig. 9). The occupation is pleasing and instructive, and forms employment for two grades of children.

Preparation of Materials.—1. *The Straws* used

should be coloured, to teach the primary shades and har-

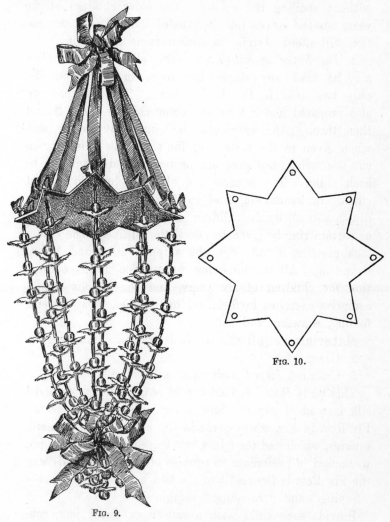

Fig. 9.

Fig. 10.

mony of combination. They must be damp when cut up into lengths to prevent their splitting. If stood on end over steam the heat penetrates, and they are easily cut without spoiling the colour. The older children of six years cut the straws into lengths of 1 inch. This occupation will afford exercise in measurement and cutting.

2. *The Paper or Silk Discs.*—The silk or paper discs may be made any shape, but round or square are the only two used in the babies' room. These shapes are also prepared and cut by the older children, who thread them through the centre upon a string ready for use, and when given to the little ones for threading it is easy to cut the string, and give six or ten threaded squares to each child. The squares are obtained by folding and cutting or by drawing and cutting. The circles may be drawn and cut by the children in the same way, if a penny or curtain ring be given to pencil the outline. The circles look prettier if the edges be snipped all round before threading. All the foregoing preparation forms occupation for children of six years, and the lessons should comprise exercises in form, colour, number, measurement, folding, drawing, and cutting.

Materials required.—1. Red straws in 1 in. lengths.

2. Green glass beads.

3. Coloured frayed inch squares of silk.[1]

This "Fly Rest" is made up of small squares of frayed silk instead of paper. Silk is not necessary, but as the Fly Rest in Fig. 9 was made in the babies' room, the silk squares, which had the edges first frayed out by the babies, were used in preference to squares of paper. In this way the Fly Rest is the result of the two babies' occupations—"fraying" and "threading" combined.

Provide each child with a saucer or small box con-

---

[1] One hundred cuttings of silk may be obtained for 1s., and last for a year.

taining ten beads, ten straws, and ten squares of paper or silk, and a neatly-knotted string half yard long, waxed or threaded in the ordinary needle-threaders.

Do not tie on a bead, for a small well-made knot is better, and will be hidden by the bow of ribbon. Ordinary balls of shop twine, or macramé thread, may be used for the threading with satisfaction.

Threading.—Children and teacher work together until strings are finished, thus :

1. Show string in right hand, and hold the needle or end in position between finger and thumb.

2. Take a bead in left hand. Thread, and let it rest upon the knot.

3. Take a square, thread and rest upon the bead.

4. Take a straw, thread and rest upon the square.

Repeat, 2, 3, 4, till all are used.

Of course, the children must previously have had a lesson upon a square, and during the threading a conversation about the colour, shape, etc., of the different things should be kept up.

Preparation by Teacher.—The "fly rest" is mounted upon an eight-pointed star (see Fig. 10), cut in stout card-board, and enamelled on both sides in pale green. At each point a small hole is punched or burnt with a hot knitting-needle, and through each hole a string is threaded. Eight or sixteen strings are required if one be added at the angles as well.

As the children finish their strings the teacher might temporarily thread them upon the star, and tell children what she is about to make with them. Talk about flies, how they are attracted by hanging things and bright colours, and this pretty article is to keep them away from troubling us, etc.

The strings are threaded through each point of the star, and finished by a bead and a knot. A crimson ribbon is sewn to each knot, and joined at the top and finished with a full bow.

The lower ends are drawn together and fastened with a bow of ribbon.

The threading of straws, paper, and beads on long strings and festooned across the room is very pleasing to the little ones. The strings are easily joined to any length.

XII. A DOUBLE KNOT AND BEAD ON SINGLE STRING.

1. Tie a knot at the half, and then tie again in the same place, making the second tie come upon the first.

2. Hold the centre double knot in the left hand and begin to make another double knot in the same manner.

3. Hold the last knot made each time when making the next, this will give equal distances between the knots.

4. Turn and knot the other half of string in similar manner.

Fig. 11.

XIII. A DOLL'S BEAD CURTAIN.

Materials required.—1. Macramé string (green) cut into ¾ yard lengths.

2. Tin or wooden saucer.

3. Twelve red beads for each child.

4. A string and threader.

Lesson.—The children delight to make something for dolly, and this exercise is very suitable, because all the children can be employed at the same work, and complete the entire curtain in one lesson. The colour of the macramé string and beads combined make a very effective combination. Red and green are Nature's colours, red flowers and green leaves. Speak of the colours and let children name as many flowers of a red colour known to them. Distribute the strings with a bead at the bottom, resting on a knot. Each child is supplied with one string and twelve beads, and works with the teacher, as she demonstrates with large beads and cord before the class.

1. Hold bead that is on the string between finger and thumb of left hand.

2. Pass the string round first finger and tie a single tie-knot.

3. Hold bead firmly and tighten knot. The knot will be about 1 inch away from the bead, if done in this way.

4. Thread a red bead to rest upon the knot. Repeat these exercises of making a knot and threading a bead until about 3 or 4 inches of the string remains.

Turn down the end about 2 inches, and tie a single

knot in the doubled strings to form a loop, and cut the end off short and neat. At this stage the teacher should collect the strings, and by means of a wire or finer string

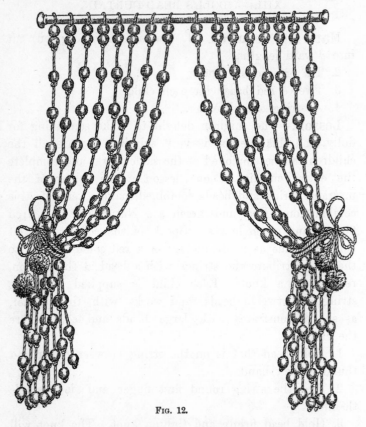

FIG. 12.

thread upon the looped end of the string two beads to rest upon the knot, so that the beads will fit closely to the stick and make a nice heading for the curtain.

Making of Curtains.—Having sufficient strings of knots and beads from the children, proceed to make the curtain before the class as the strings are finished. Talk about windows, their use, why we use blinds and curtains, etc., all the time the making is going on.

An ordinary wooden knitting pin or round stick of 6 inches in length answers for the pole. Thread the point through the loops, and when sufficient, add the end of another knitting pin to make both ends alike.

If there be no doll's house in which to place the curtain, draw a window upon a sheet of stiff cardboard, and fix the blind in position, and tie back with ribbon or loops of string as in illustration. Short blinds for the school-room windows are easily made in the same way, and are very charming in effect, because the sunlight glistens through the glass beads, and throws a subdued pretty-coloured shadow in the room.

XIV. A KNOTTED BEAD CORNICE.

Long and short curtains for the school, or window cornices may be made of knots and beads. If the beads and knots are of a contrasting shade most beautiful effects can be obtained. The clear glass or crystal bead is the best for the purpose, because the sunshine glistening through the coloured glass has a charming effect in the interior of a room. The blinds made in this way are not only useful and ornamental but a saving of labour, for they need no washing, are strong, and form an excellent means of shading a room or hiding an unsightly view without darkening the same.

The teacher must procure two flat blind-sticks, or bars of wood, the length required to fit the window, and $\frac{3}{4}$ of an inch in thickness. The top bar is to be pierced with

holes along the centre about an inch apart. These may
be drilled with a red-hot knitting-needle or gimlet. The
second bar is drilled in the same way, but with holes
½ an inch apart. These bars should be enamelled by
one of the older boys and put away until the strings are
ready to tie on.

Threading Colours (Peacock blue strings and amber beads).
—If possible get each child a small box in which to keep

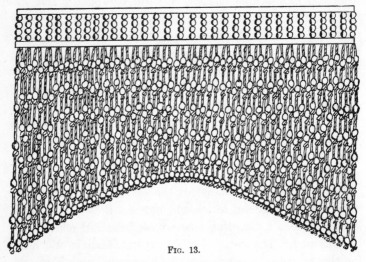

FIG. 13.

his strings and beads. Many suitable for the purpose
can be had for the asking of any draper. Cut the string
into two-yard lengths, and give one to each child. Give
twenty amber beads and let children thread and knot as
in the doll's curtain, only in this case they will begin with
a double knot and not a loop.

When sufficient lengths are nearly done it is well to
begin to make up the curtain before the little ones.

Mounting.—Take the lower bar, that is the one with

the greater number of holes, and rest it upon two nails
in the wall or across the backs of two chairs, and as every
two strings are obtained from the children thread the
ends up through two consecutive holes, and temporarily
tie together until all are threaded.

Insertion. —This part may be varied and made to represent diamonds and other patterns, according to the
skill of the worker, but as Stage I. is written for young
children a simple insertion of beads is all that is taught.
Rest the bar across the backs of two chairs and let a few
of the quickest workers come out and finish, or the bar
could be placed upon the desk in front of six such children.
The teacher must take every two strings and wax them
well together to make a firm smooth string. Six beads
are threaded upon each waxed doubled string, and then
threaded through a hole in the top bar by the children.
Of course, the first string must be threaded through the first
hole of the bar, and so on in regular order until the bar is
full. The strings of first and second holes are tied together
by a flat knot upon the top, then the third and fourth,
and fifth and sixth, and so on. A small tin tack or gimp
pin might be nailed through each knot to keep it close
to the bar. When the cornice is used, the top bar will
not be seen, and this is the only way of mounting the
strings when the whole class is engaged in making the
work, but when the occupation is undertaken by older
children who are able to manage the whole then the strings
will be threaded down double from the top. The bottom
may be straight or curved as in illustration, but this part
is easily put right when all else is done, by either untying to lengthen, or tying additional knots to shorten
where required.

A very simple, yet effective pattern, is to thread a

diamond shape in a bright distinctive colour for the diamonds, and choose a dark or black bead for the ground colour. The pattern can be done by counting the number of beads in a pattern, thus in a diamond pattern illustrated it requires seven beads and seven strings to complete. a diamond, and thus the pattern can be increased to any number of diamonds in length and width by simply multiplying the number by seven.

> Row 1. Three black, one red, three black.
> Row 2. Two black, three red, two black.
> Row 3. One black, five red, one black.
> Row 4. Seven red.
> Row 5. Same as third.
> Row 6. Same as second.
> Row 7. Same as first. Repeat 2—7.

XV. A DOUBLE KNOT ON TWO STRINGS. (See Fig. 14.)

This exercise is the same as Ex. XII. with this difference, that the knot is made each time with two strings instead of one.   This knot is largely used in Stages I. and III. in making the cords and picots for the macramé lace. The children should not be allowed to tighten their knots until examined by the teacher.   If these double knots be kept moderately loose and flat the strings, when finished, may be used as a trimming for outlining traced patterns, and have the appearance of a knotted braided gimp.

XVI. A DOUBLE KNOT ON TWO STRINGS, WITH BEADS.
(See Fig. 15.)

As a supplementary exercise to the preceding one a glass bead might be threaded on each string separately after the double knot, and by holding both beads to-

gether the strings could again be knotted as before. A
single knot could be made on each string after the bead

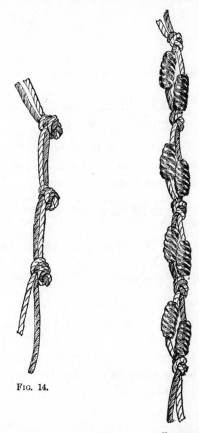

Fig. 14.

Fig. 15.

to keep it in position, and then the double knot with
both strings. These chains of beads and knots may also
be used for curtains.

XVII.   A SINGLE TIE KNOT OF THREE STRINGS.

FIG. 16.

XVIII.   A SINGLE TIE KNOT OF THREE STRINGS, WITH CENTRE BEAD. (SEE FIG. 16.)

1. Give three strings 1 yard in length, two brown and one pink.

2. Knot the ends of all three together with a single tie knot, and keep the pink string as the centre one.

3. Make a single knot on all three strings, or

3*a*. Thread a glass lozenge-shaped bead upon the centre string, and then a double knot immediately under it.

4. Take all three strings and knot together.   Repeat until the strings are used up, then use as fringe for bracket, or if knotted with macramé twine and small beads the chains may be used as a gimp trimming.

LOOP CHAIN AND PLAITING.

XIX. A FLAT KNOT FOR JOINING TWO LOOPS.

1. Give two strings of different colours, white and red, 1 yard in length. Double each string in half.

2. Take the loop ends in either hand (white in right), and pass the white loop over the red loop.

3. Pull up the ends of white string through the loop of red which is on the right (Fig. 17).

Fig. 17.

4. Pull all four ends tightly.

Use.—This knot is used for beginning the cords which are made of four knotted strings.

XX. SINGLE LOOP CHAIN OF ONE STRING.

This exercise is simply the ordinary loop chain made in crochet work, but made with the fingers without the aid of a needle.   The chain is easily undone, and the

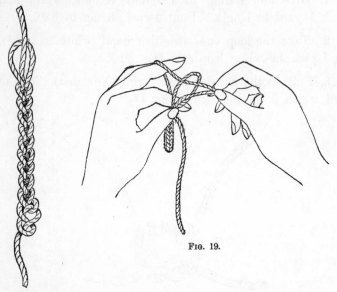

Fig. 19.

Fig. 18.

same string used again until the children are expert in the exercise.

1. Give strings 1 yard in length.   Turn down about an inch and tie a knot in the double strings (Ex. vi.) to form a loop.

2. Hold the knot between the thumb and finger of left hand, with the loop standing up, and the string hanging loosely across the fingers (Fig. 19).

3. With finger and thumb of right hand pull the string through the loop to form another loop.

4. Pull the new loop until the previous one is tight. To do this quickly pull the part of loop nearest the knot outwards.

XXI. DOUBLE LOOP CHAIN, OR KNOTTED CORD OF TWO STRINGS.

Materials required.—Two strings of contrasting shades (pink and green).

1. Knot the ends together (Ex. VI.) Take the knot in left hand and pass one string round the finger as if going to tie a single knot, but instead of pulling the whole string through the loop round the finger only pull through sufficient to form a loop.

2. Hold the cord as described in previous exercise, between the finger and thumb of left hand with the loop upright and outwards, and its string hanging down. Place the other string across the fingers and keep them spread apart.

3. Put finger and thumb of right hand through the loop and pull up the string which lies across the fingers. The loop will always be one colour, and the string to be pulled through the other.

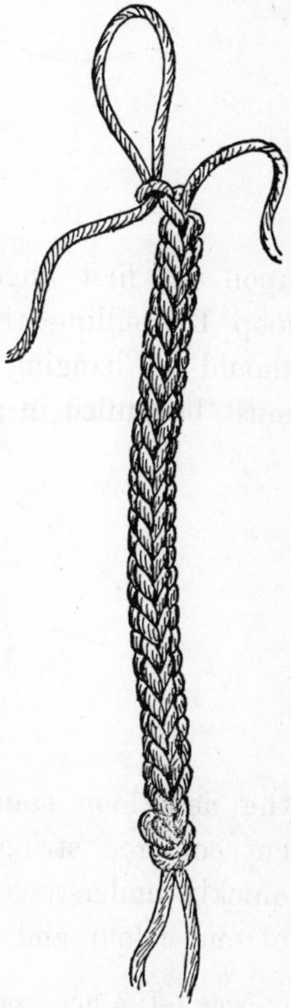

Note.—The children are apt to twist the loop or put their fingers in behind the loop and thus get an irregular cord. To obviate this fault compare the loop to an eye-glass and tell the children to

FIG. 20.

look through it, and then tell them their fingers are to go through the loop the same way that they looked through and not from the back, but straight before them through the front.

4. Pull through the new loop long enough to place

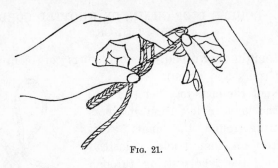

FIG. 21.

upon the first finger of left hand, and tighten the new loop by pulling the string of the previous loop, which should be hanging on the right-hand side. This string must be pulled in an oblique direction to the right until

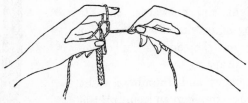

FIG. 22.

the new loop stands erect in position. If two different coloured strings are used as directed this point is quickly understood, because the loop on the finger will be of one colour and the tightening string will be the other.

Note.—If a long cord is to be worked, the string must be wound on reels or in balls, and kept fixed with a pin, otherwise, in turning the cord, the strings will get twisted.

The exercise may also be worked by both hands, looping alternately, but the best and regular work is obtained by using the right hand throughout, as described.

5. The tightening string should be held in the right hand, the loop slipped off the finger, and the cord turned over from right to left. This is done by keeping hold of the tightening string and carrying to the left across the fingers in position with the loop outwards as in illustration. When the children understand the turn of the cord they might work simultaneously from commands, thus :

1. Show work in position. Loop on right, its string hanging down. Second string across fingers.

2. Put finger and thumb through loop and raise a new loop, and place on raised fore-finger.

3. Pull string on right till loop is tightened.

4. Slip out finger, turn cord, and carry string across fingers in position for next loop. Repeat.

As the teacher gives the number the children should repeat what is to be done.

XXII. SIMPLE PLAIT OF THREE STRINGS.

This exercise is good for teaching the use of harmony of colours, and for employing the left hand equally with the right.

Materials required.—For each child, three coloured strings, $\frac{1}{2}$ a yard in length.

Lesson.—The plait may be worked loosely lying flat upon the desk, but it is better for the strings to be attached to the desk or slipped over a hook as required in Stage II. exercises. One child might hold the end of strings, whilst another plaits the same.

Colours for the first lesson.—Crimson, green, and brown.

To accustom children to the different colours call upon
them to show the individual colours when
named by the teacher, and question upon
each colour, *e.g.*, show red string. Now name
anything you know of this colour. Flowers—
poppy, geranium, roses, etc. Soldier's coat,
sun, fire, etc. Talk about each colour in a
similar manner.

Plaiting commands.—1. Place strings straight
down upon desk in order, red, green, brown.

2. Take red string and cross it over centre
one (green). The red will now be in the
centre.

3. Take brown string and cross from left
over the centre one (red). The brown will
now be the centre string.

The teacher should work before the class,
and simplify the exercise into two steps, making children understand that it is the right
and left string in turn which crosses the
centre string and so becomes the centre string

Fig. 23.

itself. In this way all the strings in turn are used.

XXIII.   PLAIT OF THREE WITH DOUBLE STRINGS.
(SEE FIG. 24.)

XXIV.   PLAIT OF THREE WITH TRIPLE STRINGS.

These plaits are worked exactly like Ex. XXII., only
that more strings are used. The double or triple strings
must be laid perfectly flat when plaiting.

XXV. DUSTING-BRUSH OF PLAITED AND FRAYED STRINGS.

Long plaits may be made by the children and used for ornamenting the edges of pockets, tidies, picture-frames,

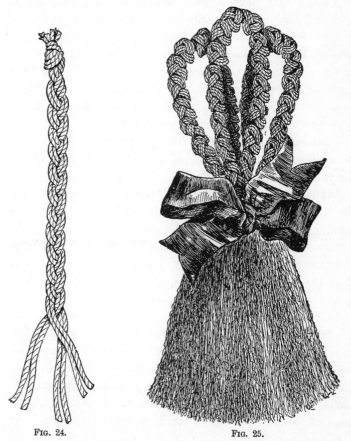

FIG. 24.   FIG. 25.

etc. One pretty and useful way of using these long plaits is to make an ornament dusting brush (see Fig. 25) for the small knick-knacks of the drawing-room.

Cut three pieces of Manilla rope $\frac{1}{2}$ a yard long. Tie round each piece a twist of cotton about 2 inches from the ends. Let the children untwist the ends and fray each separate coil into threads.

Take a long plait of nine strings, and after leaving an end of 3 inches tie the plait to the rope over the twist of cotton. Wind the plait evenly round the rope to completely cover it, and then tie the other end over the twist of cotton in the same way as the first. The loose ends of the plait are cut the same length as the frayed rope and untwisted and frayed to cover one side of the rope ends. Three or four pieces of rope and plaited string are needed to make a full brush, and will form a good occupation for a large class as different children could be preparing different parts.

When the ropes are finished as described, each rope is doubled in half and tied together, the loop ends form the handle, but the ropes could be plaited or twisted for the handle before being tied together if desired. The loops must be wound VERY TIGHTLY just above the frayed part with thread or macramé twine, and the join covered with a bow of ribbon to match the strings.

Comb all the fraying with a fine comb and see that the frayed strings are uppermost all round the brush. Cut the bottom even and show the class the dusting-brush which they have made, its use, colour, materials, etc. These brushes may be made in the babies' room of rope alone, but the coloured strings add much to the appearance of the article, and so make it more educational and pleasing to children.

XXVI. A FLAT AMBULANCE OR REEF KNOT FOR JOINING TWO STRINGS.

This knot is used for tying bandages, and in all cases where a flat and secure knot is needed. It is a most essential knot for children to learn, and the teacher might make the lesson very interesting by bandaging a child's head or arm and showing how flat and securely the knot rests in position, and then by showing the difference by tying a double knot in the usual fashion (Ex. VI.).

To make the knot easily understood distribute two

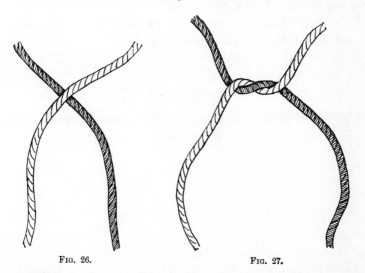

FIG. 26.   FIG. 27.

strings of different colours (red and white), about ½ a yard in length.

Commands.—1. Take one end of red string in right hand, and white in left.

2. Hold each about 1 inch from the end, and cross keeping red under the white (Fig. 26).

3. Hold the cross with thumb and finger of right hand and twist red end over and under the white string (Fig. 27). Draw the attention of the children to the fact that the strings have changed their positions, the red has travelled from the right to the left but it will have to come back again to complete the knot. Also point out that the right-hand string which starts *under* the white must maintain that position throughout. It is now on the left hand but still *under* the white string.

4. Draw ends outwards and then recross for return journey. Call upon children to say how the red string must travel. Under the white.

5. Pass red string back under and over the white string and pull both strings tightly (Fig. 28).

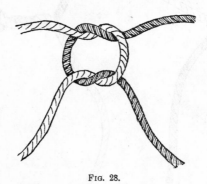

Fig. 28.

Use.—This knot is used in joining the strings for knotting, because it can be pulled very small and tight, and worked as to be almost unnoticeable.

Note.—It is best to keep the children's attention fixed upon the movement of the right-hand string (red) only, when the knot will become quite simple.

XXVII. OPEN GIMP OF FLAT KNOTS.

To give practice in this knot pass the strings over a hook fastened in the desk (Fig. 29), and let the children tie round a short stick each time until perfect. If the two colours be used the teacher or child will easily discover when the knot is wrong, which can be untied before others are made.

This open gimp is useful for ornamentation, and can be made any length by putting the loops over the hook from time to time. Ribbon can be threaded through the loops and drawn up to make serviette rings, or several lengths, if crocheted together and ribbon interlaced in alternate ones, may be used as antimacassars.

Fig. 29.

CORDS WORKED ON KNOTTING FRAME No. 1.

KNOTTING FRAME No. 1.

The exercises in this book have all been worked with just the simple appliances mentioned, which were adapted to meet the exigencies of the work, but the writer found by practical experience that better work could more easily be obtained if suitable helps were provided. To meet these wants two knotting frames have been designed by the writer for that purpose.

In several of the cords in Stage I., a support for the

cord is needed, and an empty cotton reel was made to answer the purpose. By this arrangement the child had to give up the use of its left hand entirely to hold the reel, and only with Ex. XXVIII. could this plan answer efficiently, because, in making the other cords, both hands are needed and the reel must rest on the desk. This

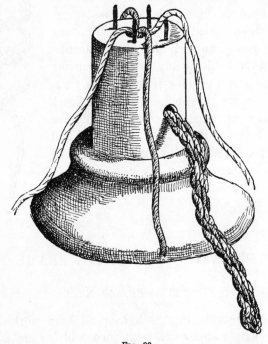

Fig. 30.

could be done at first, but as the cord increased in length and protruded through the hole of the reel, the reel could not stand without being held by the hand and thus the child had to cope with a difficulty which is avoided with suitable appliances.

No. 1 Knotting Frame meets all these difficulties :

1. It is designed as a reel upon a circular base, which is sufficiently large to stand firmly in position and afford a rest for the two hands when working.

2. The frame is circular and hollowed out inside large enough for the child's fingers to enter. Just above the base a small hole is drilled for the cord to pass through as it is worked, and by this arrangement the stability of the base is not interfered with. The cord passes out in view of the child, who is pleased at seeing its work increase, and the cords may be wound round the frame or be received in a small bag and kept clean.

3. The top of frame has four small pins inserted at right angles round the hole. These headless pins are needed for Ex. XXVIII. upon which to work the loops, and in the successive exercises they are used for placing or holding the strings in position.

In the spiral cord the strings are placed between the pins, and in the square cord they are carried across and wound round the pins once, and thus held in position till the last cord is threaded through the loop of the first.

Similar in construction to this cord is frame knitting, so called because it is worked upon a pegged frame.

These frames may be had in various sizes, and the one most suitable for macramé string is Mrs. Hibbert's scarf frame, at 1s. 9d. each. Upon these frames bags, curtain bands, cushion covers, etc., can be made.

For curtain bands work a length of knitting about ¾ yard in length, fasten off, and draw each end up tightly and add a button-holed brass ring.

For a bag, crochet the bottom straight across on the wrong side, and turn down a hem at the top and sew with twine.

The bag can be lined with a bright colour and used quite flat, or it may be drawn up with small rings attached at the top.

Deep shopping bags may be worked loosely on these frames.

All the cords worked on the No. 1 Frame are suitable for "draw strings" or "handles" to the bags.

The bags may be worked in two or more colours according to taste, or a band of colour can be worked in at the top as a border.

The principle of working is the same as the cord, the string is twisted round each peg loosely and then lifted over the peg and string with the finger to form a second loop.

XXVIII. A ROUND CORD OF CHAIN STITCHES.

This exercise is simply the old-fashioned reel work so much enjoyed by boys in making reins in coloured wools.

Materials required.—1. Large cotton reels, or drilled ribbon-rollers, or wooden blind-rollers, either of which are suitable, or Knotting Frame No. 1.

2. Macramé thread No. 10.

3. Gimp pins and blanket pins.

Prepare the reels or rollers by fixing in four short headless nails or gimp pins, and twist the thread loosely once round each pin. In doing this, let the thread pass inside the pin first and then round and across to next nail.

To work, the reel is held in left hand and the string held above and across each loop on the pegs. The right hand with blanket pin lifts up the lower loop over the thread which forms a new loop. Each loop is worked in turn, and the cord increases and passes down through the hole of the reel. The cord resembles four chain stitches joined together as in Ex. xx.

If the cord be worked in one colour a spiral centre for mat may be made of it, or reins, or watch-guards. When a cord the length required is finished take off the four stitches from pegs, and with crochet needle finish each off separately or pull a loop through all four stitches at once.

XXIX. A SPIRAL CORD OF TWO COLOURS.

This is a very pretty cord, simple to do and has a spiral effect. It may be worked in the hands at first, but as the work increases in length it is better to have some support to hold it. A large reel upon which silk twist has been wound is the kind of reel best to hold the cord because of its size, although any ordinary reel would do. As many of the cords described in this Stage require similar support. It is best to obtain a number of wooden rollers from a draper, and with stock and bit to drill the holes about as large as a threepenny bit.

Lesson.—Give each child two strings of different colours, 1 yard each in length. Select two colours that harmonize well, such as pink and green, or blue and yellow. Talk about the colours and the measurements of a yard whilst distributing the strings.

The aim of the lesson is to teach what is meant by a right angle. The blackboard must be largely used to illustrate the position of the string.

1. Take the blue string and place to form an upright or vertical line on the desk, draw the line it makes on blackboard and hastily inspect the class.

2. Take the yellow string and place across the blue string to form a cross and horizontal line upon it. Sketch

the diagram on blackboard and give the terms East, West, North, South, and show how each string runs in a different direction and no two of them would ever meet. Explain that if two lines form a corner of a square as these lines meet in the centre, they are said to be. at right angles (Fig. 31). Show the corners of the blackboard, the table, the door, in illustration of what is meant, and sketch several angles on blackboard, and let the children determine which are right angles.

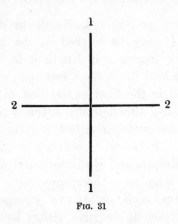

FIG. 31

The ground work being fully understood begin to teach the cord. The basis of which is simply tying a single tie-knot across at right angles to the last, alternately. The blue string is under, therefore take the top and lower end of the blue and tie across the yellow, and pull both ends back to the top and bottom in the same position as at first. Next take the right and left ends of the yellow strings and tie across the knot just tied by the blue strings. In the progress of working, the cord twists itself and when finished will appear like a spiral of blue and yellow knots of very pretty design (Fig. 32). The advantage of having two colours is palpable, the children know which two strings to tie which they would not if all were alike. Only about 1 inch can be worked without a support, and after the first lesson the exercise should be continued by either fixing the cord in the hole of a reel, or attaching the end to a hook in the desk. The cord need not be made in long lengths as it is easily joined.

FIG. 32.

When the child has learned to keep the strings respectively right and left, and north and south as they are tied then the most proficient might venture to make gentlemen's watch-guards in silk cord or Russia braid. The guards should be rather more than a $\frac{1}{4}$ of a yard long and have swivel and hook attached when finished.

XXX. A SQUARE KNOTTED CORD OF FOUR STRINGS.

This cord is very suitable for watch-guards when made in black silk cord or Russia braid (Fig. 38). It is very

simple and is made of four strings.   For a first lesson it is
best to have the four strings of a different colour so that

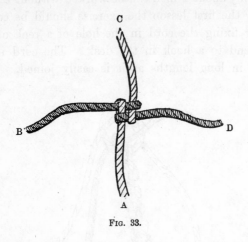

FIG. 33.

definite commands can be given and followed by the
children.   The cord, when finished, is square or four-sided,

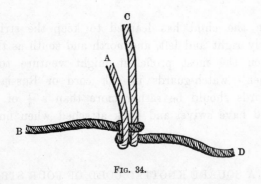

FIG. 34.

and is made by crossing every string at right angles to
the last.   Give the children a clear idea of what is meant

by crossing at right angles, and illustrate the position of strings on blackboard.

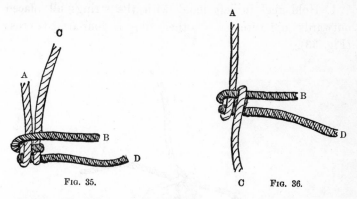

FIG. 35.   FIG. 36.

Materials for each child.— A large reel or ribbon-roller with hole in centre, or Knotting Frame No. 1.

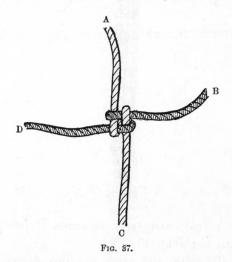

FIG. 37.

Four strings of different colours knotted together (Ex. VI.), and inserted in the hole.

We will suppose that the four strings are red, white, blue, and brown.

1. Hold reel in left hand with the strings all placed outwards opposite each other like a four-armed cross (Fig. 33).

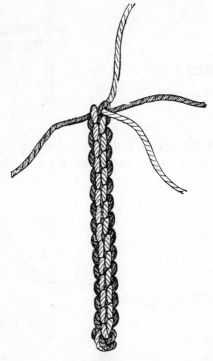

FIG. 38.

2. Take A (red) and carry it across B (white) to lie parallel with C (blue) (Fig. 34).

3. Take B (white) and carry it across A and C to lie parallel with D (brown) (Fig. 35).

4. Bring C across B to take position of A (Fig. 36).

5. Carry D over C and thread through the loop formed by A at starting (Fig. 37).

This completes one half of the process, and it will be noticed that the starting position of each string is shifted from left to right, therefore to regain the first position the strings are again crossed similar as before, only in this half they start from the right-hand side as it were, working backwards when the strings will be in the same position as at first.

The children will soon learn that each string goes straight across to the opposite side in turn, and the last one is threaded through the loop of the first. The children must hold the strings down between the fingers of left hand whilst working, but at first the reel can be rested upon the desk and both hands left free to work, when the strings can be managed without difficulty.

XXXI. WALL POCKET, TRIMMED WITH KNOTTED CORDS.

This pretty little pocket is trimmed with the double loop chain cord (Fig. 39). A small cardboard shaped pocket, consisting of two pieces with side gussets, is cut out and covered in cheap velveteen and neatly oversewn round the edges by the children. The cord is looped on the front and lower portion of the pocket as seen in illustration, and sewn all round the edge as a trimming. The colours used are pink and fawn strings. The pocket is covered in pink velveteen at $6\frac{3}{4}$d. per yard, and lined with cheap pink sateen. One yard of sateen at $4\frac{1}{2}$d. will make a dozen linings, and two yards of the velveteen will cover as many fronts. The velveteens for this purpose may be obtained at any fancy draper's, who often will put remnants and soiled silks, etc., at a great reduction. The "making up" is a valuable occupation for girls to exercise their neatness in sewing.

Fig. 39.

BUTTON-HOLE KNOTTING ON RINGS.

XXXII.   SIMPLE BUTTON-HOLE STITCH ON BRASS RINGS.

Simple button-hole stitch is a very useful stitch to learn at an early stage, as it enters largely into every pattern and kind of knot, and is really the foundation of the macramé knot. It is best to teach button-hole knot upon a foundation, and for this purpose brass curtain-rings have been found very suitable as they are small and light and easily held by the children.

Supply a small ball of string and a brass ring to each child and work with them as follows :

1. Hold the ring in left hand with the end of string under the left thumb until a few stitches are worked, when the end may be let loose. (Leave an end of six inches.)

2. With ball of string in right hand make a hanging loop, and pass the ball down through the ring and out through the loop.

3. Pull the ball outwards till the stitch fits the ring, and keep the button-hole edge outwards and even throughout, and all the stitches close and regular.

The children are apt to tighten the stitches too much; they look best if worked moderately tight and even, and will more easily be joined together.

When the rings are full the string should be threaded through the edge of the first stitch and fastened off on the under side, or the ends tied together and used for joining to other rings.

XXXIII. SIMPLE BUTTON-HOLE ON FINGERS.

When the children understand the stitch they might make rings or loops of button-hole stitches upon the fingers.

Give two strings of *different* colours, and name one the foundation string and the other the working string. The working string is the one with which the knots are made.

The foundation string need not be as long as the working one.

1. Hold the foundation string tightly across the fingers of the left hand, and compare it to the brass ring.

2. Begin and work several stitches upon the foundation string just as directed in previous exercise, and when twenty stitches or less have been worked the children could draw them up tightly to form scallops or rings. The foundation string is joined round to the first stitch. After each scallop knot the two strings together with a single knot and begin again. If desired the strings could change places, and alternate scallops of the two colours could be worked after the single knot. The pattern somewhat resembles the shape of shells, and will be useful for trimming mats and tidies.

XXXIV.   BUTTON-HOLED RING WITH FILLED CENTRE.

The button-hole rings are much improved by filling in the centres, but as needle and twine and a variety of stitches can be used for this part of the work the filling in of centres has been reserved for Stage II. The exercise can be worked with the one string throughout, and therefore it is taken for Stage I. When the ring is fully button-holed pass the string through the edge of first stitch and make ring complete. An ordinary bodkin or needle threader will be needed for working the centre. Pass the string across to the other side of the ring under two stitches and recross to the other side. Pass under three stitches and cross over and return as in illustration. There will be three strings tightened across the centre of ring widening towards the lower side. With the same string the child now weaves to and fro across the three strings until the centre is filled. This will bring mat plaiting into use. Finish the ring by passing the string

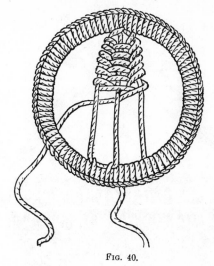

FIG. 40.

under a few stitches at the back, or leave end for joining to other rings.

XXXV. A WALL POCKET OF RINGS.

The rings worked in preceding exercise may be utilized in many ways, one of which is the wall-pocket in illustration. Having obtained thirty-six worked rings from the class, join the same neatly together to form a triangle, beginning with a row of eight and decreasing one ring in each row.

To join the rings together use a carpet needle and macramé thread of the same colour as the string. Keep the under side of the rings uppermost and sew across the stitches, taking care to leave the button-hole edge intact. The right side will show the rings edge to edge but no unsightly joins.   Cut out two triangular shapes

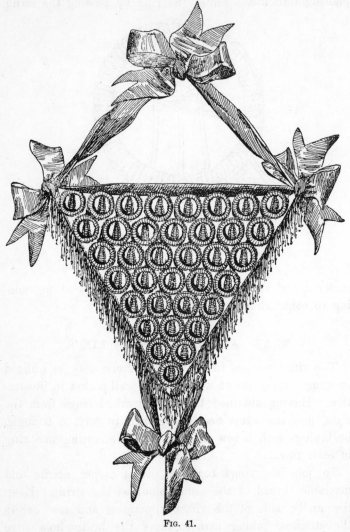

FIG. 41.

in cardboard about an inch larger every way than the

triangle of rings. See that the shape is perfect and true, and the lower corner exactly in the centre. Both these pieces have to be covered with sateen on both sides to form the outer and inner lining of the pocket. If nicely placed and tacked each piece can be oversewn separately in cotton of same colour by a girl of seven years.

To make the pocket more capacious and useful two side pieces or gussets may be inserted; these also are cut in cardboard, and the sides must measure in length the sides of front triangular pieces. About 4 inches wide at the top is sufficient, but the side pieces may be wider or narrower according to fancy.

Let children cover and oversew these in sateen to match the larger pieces.

There are now four triangular pieces prepared for the pocket—two equilateral triangles for back and front of pocket, and two long triangular side pieces.

Take the back of pocket and join on the two side pieces. See that they exactly fit from point to top. Pin together and let a child closely oversew both sides.

The front of pocket is decorated with the rings, and the work is more effective if the front of pocket is covered with cheap velveteen instead of sateen before the rings are laid on.

The pocket in illustration is made of tan-brown worked rings, mounted upon royal blue velveteen, and finished with ribbons of the same colour. Of course, pockets, and bags, and mats, and curtain-bands may be made of rings only, simply joined together without any foundation or lining.

Curtain-band.—Join twenty-four worked rings together in twelve pairs and attach a single worked ring at either end.

STAGE II.

INTRODUCTION.

THIS Stage consists of knots and bars made of two or more strings upon other strings or firm foundations. Ordinary brass curtain-rings, or a cheaper make used for ring-laying, can be used for this occupation at little expense. The rings impart a firmness to the work that is unattainable by any other means, and they are not seen as the knotting completely covers the foundation. Any of the knots made of one or two strings are suitable for ring work, and the twisted ones are especially pretty and liked by the children. The rings are light and easily worked in the hand and the centres may be filled in various ways with needle and thread of a finer make. The skilful workers might use the cardboard moulds which are sold at a penny to twopence per dozen, or dressmakers' small steel dress-rings are very suitable. The moulds may be had in various shapes, but round or pear-shaped is best as the corners need careful treatment, which the little ones do not manage well. The moulds and steel rings are light and do not add much to the weight of the work, but have the effect of imparting a raised appearance to the outline and prominent parts of the pattern. They are worked in the fine twine or linen thread or silk, and very pretty and useful articles may be made of the rings. The occupation is one much enjoyed by careful little girls of seven years of age who are good at needle-work. If the mould has a corner or point, that should be the place to begin.

The covered milliners' wire is also very good for foundations of this Stage because the wire may be obtained in any colour, and in any size and at little cost, the knotting is worked upon it in a straight position like upon a cord, but can be bent to any shape when finished and maintain that position. Copper, zinc, and other cheap wires may be used for the close knots, and also coarse cane; cardboard and strips of wood and rope make foundations, in fact anything that is firm and pliable can be covered with knotting and manipulated into most pretty and artistic shapes without much trouble.

Children of capability might cover the moulds with coloured crochet cotton and bone crochet hook. The simple chain is easy and gives a nice edge to the work, and is useful for joining the rings together. The fine macramé thread has a smooth glossy surface and is manufactured in a variety of beautiful art shades, and with a little thought very pleasing combinations can be produced.

To present one difficulty at the time is the object of this book, and therefore the knots of this Stage are arranged under two heads, viz.: "Knots with a fixed foundation," and "Knots in which the foundation strings are held."

Knotting Frame.—For teaching both kinds of knots in this Stage an old slate frame has been found to answer the purpose. The great advantage of having a frame is in giving each child its own work free from tangles, and

in no need of any preparation, because, if the frames
are properly prepared at first, the one preparation will
last the class for quite three months before the whole
of them are at the same level of efficiency. The plan
of working is, to teach every *new* exercise to the whole
class at the same time, and, as a large percentage
of sharp children will naturally finish before the less
clever ones, these are kept employed at useful supplementary work consisting of the *same* knots which they
have completed on their frames. The teacher knows they
are proficient in the exercise and can therefore give her
attention to the backward ones and bring them up to
the level of the others ready to learn a new exercise.

The great advantage of the frame is, that it avoids the
necessity of tying and untying foundation cords every
lesson, which only get hopelessly entangled unless very
great care is taken when collecting. The supplementary
exercises are worked on cords and round blind-sticks
fixed across the desk, or upon wire foundations, or upon
strings attached to a hook in the desk. Each will be
described after the exercises to which they belong.

The hooks would in no way interfere with the desk
for other purposes, and would be preferable to string
because the supplementary cords can be caught on the
hook, and the child is able to pull and obtain that tightness and regularity which is so essential to the appearance
of the work. A long length of cord to over-knot will
keep a quick child well employed for some considerable
time until the others have finished their frame exercise.
The long knotted cords when completed will make spiral
centres for mats, or be used as trimming to outline the
shape of any fancy articles.

Any of the knots made on the fixed foundation cords

are suitable to make over any foundation whether it be wood or wire. The small penny gridirons or toasting racks sold at any Italian warehouse for a few pence may be knotted and turned into very useful racks or pockets. The work is made attractive and simple to the children by using different coloured strings in the exercises. The different colours not only add to the beauty and effectiveness of the exercises, but they teach taste in combining colours and enable the teacher to give a definite command for each string which a child can at once understand and follow.

The chief points to be attended to are:

1. To work each knot of equal tightness.

2. To draw each knot close up to the last before another is made.

3. To keep the edges of the flat bars even and regular.

Materials.—The *Slate Frame* must be drilled with six or eight holes, top and bottom, about an inch apart, and then strung with a double thick string or single coarse cord. The string of this foundation must be continuous and strained very tightly. Tie the end at the corner hole on the inner side of the slate, and bring the cord up through the hole, cross over to opposite hole, pass down through that hole and up through the next. Recross and continue threading "down and up" on either side until the slate is full. Twist the string round the frame and return, threading a second string in the same holes, pull all very tightly, knot securely, and cut off end. Paste a small label bearing child's name in top right-hand corner of slate, and all preparation is at an end.

KNOTTING FRAME No. 2.　(See Fig. 43.)

This frame is designed to take the place of the slate frame, and to provide advantages in which the slate frame is deficient.

Only certain slate frames will allow of holes being drilled, for some are manufactured of cross-grained woods which split immediately a hole is attempted, whilst others have iron plates inserted for strength, which will not allow holes to be drilled.　Then, again, it will only be in very large schools where any accumulation of use-less cracked and scratched slates will be found sufficient to start a class at the work, and for teachers wishing to teach macramé, it is as well that they should make a good beginning and buy the most suitable appliances.

1. The Knotting Frame No. 2 is made of a heavier wood than the slate frame because the work needs it, and the slate frames have been found too light, and easily moved and rattled because of their lightness.

2. The Knotting Frame No. 2 is made with raised ends, top and bottom, into which a bar of iron is inserted on which to tie the strings.

The slate frame being shallow, it was found that the children had little space for their fingers between the cords and the desk, hence a frequent raising and rattle of the slate was occasioned.　In the Knotting Frame No. 2 this difficulty is overcome, because the cords are raised quite 2 inches above the level of the desk, and there is ample room to use the fingers without lifting the frame.

3. No holes are needed to be drilled and thus limit the number of exercises.　The bars are strong and firmly inserted and may be used for either set of exercises with

fixed or without fixed foundations. As these exercises
are worked they may be pushed up close together on
the bars, and any number of different cords can be worked
till the bars are full.

Fig. 42.—Knotting Frame No. 2.

4 When a class has worked all the exercises then
the frame can be utilized for fringes and patterns. By

turning the frame horizontally with the bars vertical at either end, the frame becomes a small macramé board and the foundation cords are tied across from one bar

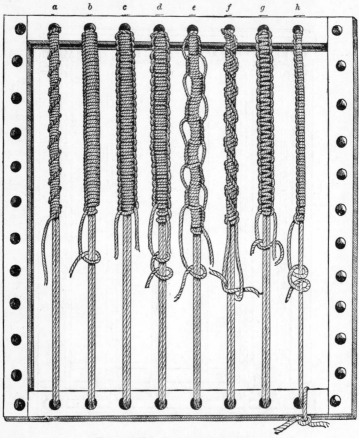

FIG. 43.—Slate Frame, with Exercises.

to the other, as on the boards used in Stage III. If a length of fringe is needed, the foundation cords should be

knotted entirely round, so that the frame may be turned
over and the work continued on the under side.

These frames may be had of the writer, or Messrs.
Charles & Dible, Paternoster Square.

The Case.—The strings get soiled if left uncovered, and
to keep the work fresh and clean large coarse brown
paper envelopes are used, in which the frame is kept.
The envelopes are sold, for cardboard materials, in packets
of twenty-five, at 1s. 6d. per packet. The envelopes
look nice, ensure tidiness, quick distribution (if labelled),
and will hold not only the frame, but also the supplementary work a child is doing. Or a teacher might let
the children make Holland or calico bags for the purpose,
which could be washed, and last for years. Again the
teacher's cupboard is free from tangled slates and strings,
and the work which needs overlooking before the next
lesson can be kept separate from the rest, and the envelopes tied together without having the whole to examine
needlessly.

A drilled slate is not necessary for the second set
of exercises, because the strings can be either tied or
looped over the frame, and as the strings are constantly
changing hands with a different foundation each time,
those children who find it easier to work might temporarily
tie the foundation string round the bottom end of frame
each time; but the arrangement will take much longer
and there is no need for it except with very stupid
children.

Another way of making the foundation is by looping
a double cord, or fixing a round blind-stick in the iron
work or inside two hooks across the desk, upon which
to knot the working strings. Any teacher who has tried
the plan of tying cords across the desk has, no doubt,

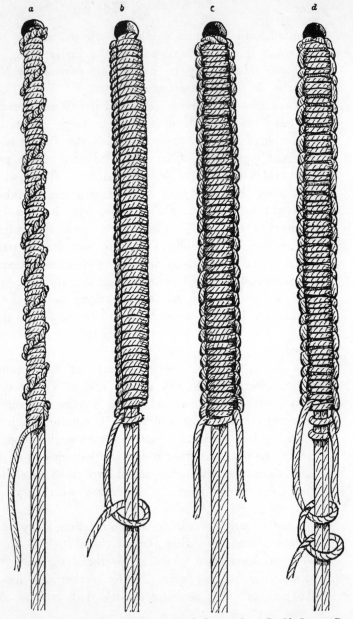

a	*b*	*c*	*d*

Corkscrew Bar.   Button-Hole Bar.   Single Genoese Bar.   Double Genoese Bar.
Fig. 43 enlarged, showing how the

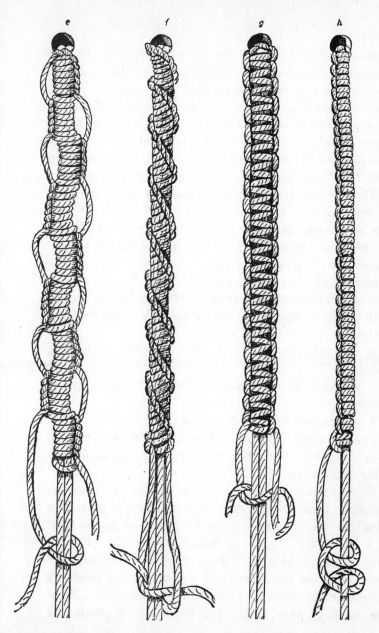

Waved or Shell Bar.　Twisted or Bannister Bar. Solomon Knot Bar.　Tatted Bar.
exercises are worked on Class Slate.

become disheartened at the preparation it entails, the tangled strings, and the unsatisfactory results produced, because the foundation lacks what it is supposed to be, viz., " a foundation." The occupation will be found to be a pleasure to both teacher and children if the suggestions in this little volume are followed and slates or knotting frames are strung for the teaching exercises, and rods and hooks used for the supplementary work.

The exercises are arranged so that both hands are made to work equally as far as possible, and any knot that can be reversed is taught for the training of both hands.

The following materials will be needed for all the exercises, so they are mentioned here and not at the beginning of every exercise :

1. A knotting frame or an old slate frame drilled with eight or nine holes about an inch apart top and bottom.

2. Coarse white macramé cord for the foundation strings.

3. A large brown paper envelope 12 inches by 10 inches.

4. A gummed label with child's name affixed.

Preliminary Lesson.—Give the above materials to each child and interest the children by talking about each thing and its use.

First the bag, and compare it to a letter or envelope. Question from the children how a letter is sent to a friend in the country. (Sent by post.) What is done to a letter that is sent by post ? (Directed.) Explain what is meant by the address, and draw an imaginary letter upon the blackboard and use one of the children's names for the address. This will interest them. What else must be done before the letter can be put in the post ? (Stamped.) Yes, it must be stamped, who can show where the stamp is fixed on a letter? Let a child come and point on blackboard or on an envelope. Having arrested the children's attention to notice the top right-hand corner of their envelopes let all put their finger on the place till teacher has hastily examined the class, and if correct, distribute the gummed labels which should have been previously prepared with each child's name.

Compare the label to a stamp, and let each child stick on its own name in the top right corner. Even with all this care there will be sure to be some who are thoughtless and put the label anywhere but where they were told, but it is not for a teacher to expect perfection at first, children come to school to be trained and taught, and if the majority of the class follow the teaching clearly at first the teacher has every reason to congratulate herself upon her teaching.

Next give out the ready strung frames, draw attention to the cords and write the word "F-o-u-n-d-a-t-i-o-n" upon the blackboard, and call upon children to pronounce it. Tell them the cords are so called because upon them the work is to be made. Compare them to the foundations of a house. All is now ready to start work and no further preparation will be needed for some months, the frames are enclosed in the envelope, the bags passed and collected ready for the first exercise.

EXERCISES UPON A FIXED FOUNDATION.

I. A BUTTON-HOLE STITCH TO THE RIGHT.

This exercise is ordinarily worked with two strings, one of which is held or fixed and the other knotted. The fixed string is always cut the length of the piece required, but the knotting string must be much longer as it soon gets used up, a small ball of string should be provided for each child about 2 yards long, sufficient to knot the whole cord on the slate without a join. Keep each ball in a little calico bag, so that the heat of the hand will not affect the gloss of the string.

Distribute balls of strings, and let each child tie the end through the hole or round the cords of first strands on slate.   Demonstrate on blackboard, and work with the children to the following commands :

1. Take string in right hand and hold outwards to the right.

2. Turn round downwards to form a loop and carry the string across the foundation cords.

3. Pass the string under the cords and draw it up through the loop.

4. Pull outwards to the right until quite tight.

This completes the knot, and the knot is repeated to " over," " under," and " through the loop," until the children are able to work unaided.

II. A BUTTON-HOLE STITCH TO THE LEFT.
(See Fig. 43 *b*, page 64.)

This exercise is the exact reverse of the preceding one.   Its object is to give dexterity to the left hand.

The bar is liable to twist if worked for more than 2 inches, therefore it is best to work Ex. I. and Ex. II. alternately on the first foundation cords to the bottom. Use a different colour for each alternate string.

In beginning on a new string simply tie the end to the cords with a single tie-knot and leave an end of 1 inch. This end must lie parallel with the foundation cords and be knotted over with them until quite hidden.

III. A TWISTED OR CORKSCREW BAR.
(SEE FIG. 43 *a*, PAGE 64.)

This exercise may be made of either the two preceding exercises. As before mentioned the button hole bars are liable to twist if worked for any length, and to get the twist uniform the string is passed back and under the foundation cords at every sixth stitch. This turn will give a pretty twist to the bar similar to the turn of a corkscrew from which it gets its name. It has been found desirable to give each knot a special name whenever possible, as it pleases and interests the children, who better remember it if compared to something familiar.

SUPPLEMENTARY EXERCISES OF I., II., AND III.

Those who have finished their frame exercise may be kept employed at the following work until the whole class have arrived at efficiency, and are able to begin a new knot.

Give the quick workers a brass ring to cover, either in button-hole or corkscrew stitch. The child can work with the string alone or use one of the needle threaders. The stitch must not be too tight, what is wanted is regularity. The children are apt to crowd the stitches and get them so tight on the ring that they are with difficulty moved into place. This tightness must be guarded against, and easy stitches, not loose and yet not tight, be aimed at. When the ring is evenly covered, thread a tapestry needle with the twine and connect the first and last stitches at the button-hole edge and fasten off underneath.

The following articles are made of rings or wire, button-holed with macramé thread or twine, which is much finer than the string, of smooth, glossy appearance, and can be had in beautiful shades. The children use the ordinary needle threaders or tapestry needles.

IV. CORKSCREW FLOWER BASKET.

The copper-wire baskets sold in the streets at a penny for flower pots answer admirably for knotting purposes. They need not be unfastened, but can be flattened out and worked as they are. If, however, all the class are to be employed in the same work, then a small pair of pliers will easily separate the parts, and the children can knot the different portions. There are nine pointed arches, one circle and two cross bars, and three wires for the handle to each basket, thus affording foundations and work for fifteen children.

In the illustration the basket is covered in corkscrew button-hole stitch, and the wires of handle in double Genoese or button-hole stitch. If the basket is taken to pieces care must be taken that the parts are correctly interlaced when joined together again.

The basket in illustration is worked in alternate points of green and yellow, with pretty effect.

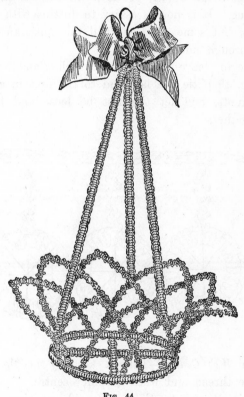

Fig. 44.

V. BRASS RING FRINGE.

The rings are the ordinary brass curtain rings which cost from 1s 6d. to 3s. per gross according to the size. They are worked in the hand without a needle and simply button-holed all round.

Method.—Give each child a ring and a small ball of
string about 2 yards in length. Wrap the ball in paper
or a small calico bag, to keep the child's fingers from
the string. It is not necessary to do this with the quick
workers, but some children spoil the appearance of their
work through hot hands.

To begin, leave an end of 6 inches and knot round
the ring, then tie the last end to the first in a series of
chain knots, and let the last be loose and both ends
tied together.

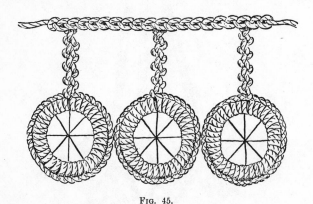

Fig. 45.

Spider Web Centre.—Take a tapestry needle and fine
macramé thread and work a spider centre.

1. Join thread to the under side of ring and cross
over at the half.

2. Thread through the under part of stitches to the
quarter, and again cross to opposite side.

3. Thread under stitches again half way and cross to
opposite side.

4. Thread from the under stitches to next quarter and
cross half way.

There will be four strands crossing in this way, and all must be caught together in the centre, when each one crosses.

The ring fringe in illustration is made of alternate rings of yellow and peacock blue. The yellow rings have blue centres, and the blue rings yellow centres.

All are crocheted together with a bone crochet hook and string of same colour.

These rings may be joined to form a variety of geometrical patterns and if different colours are used, the effect is most striking. Handsome mantel borders, curtain bands, mats, frames, bell pulls, and numerous useful furniture decorations can be made with them.

Single ones look well suspended at the curves of the gridiron and toast rack wall-pockets.

VI. RING PHOTOGRAPH FRAME.

Materials required.—1. Twenty-eight brass rings, the size of a halfpenny.

2. Macramé twine (peacock blue).

3. A tapestry needle.

4. $\frac{1}{4}$ yard cheap velveteen.

The frame measures 10 inches by 6 inches, and is cut out in firm cardboard with a centre space $4\frac{1}{2}$ inches long, and 3 inches wide. It is covered with cheap velveteen, and the rings are joined neatly together and sewn on in position. Cut a much smaller centre out of the velveteen and snip back to the corners and paste the edges over on the under side.

Mount the rings to the cardboard foundation and cut a second cardboard shape like the first, only having no centre space. Glue the second shape to the back of the

Fig. 46.

other, and leave a space at bottom in which to push the photograph. If desired, only one cardboard mount need be used, and the photograph can be slipped under the rings and kept in position.

The frame may be used for the table by adding a stand at the back, or it can be suspended by a button-holed loop as in illustration.

Filling in of ring centres.—When the ring is fully button-holed and the first and last stitch neatly joined together, keep the same thread and needle and cross over to opposite side of ring and catch to the under side of two stitches, then return to starting point again, twisting the needle round and round the first crossing thread. This twisted strand divides the ring in half.

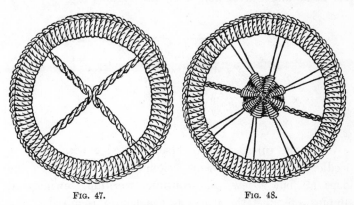

Fig. 47.   Fig. 48.

Count the stitches in each half and slip the needle under one half to the quarters of the ring (Fig. 47), and from thence cross and recross, twisting as before, but at the centre make a cross stitch to keep the crossing together. Take the filling in of the rings as a separate lesson, or the quick ones who, if taken around the teacher whilst she works one, will be able to proceed with any number of rings and teach others as they begin to learn the supplementary work.

The second ring is filled in as a double spider's web (Fig. 48), and the strands are worked with a back stitch from strand to strand.

VII. BUTTON-HOLE FRINGE.

The children well knowing the button-hole stitch might make the same over a ruler, to form loops, which can be sewn and used as a fringe.

1. Give each child a wooden 12-inch flat ruler and a small ball of string.

2. Tie the end of string to the ruler and hold it in left hand and button-hole with the right.

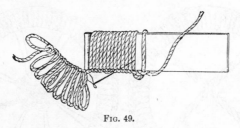

Fig. 49.

When the ruler is full, oversew the edge with tapestry needle and thread of same colour and then slip off the loops all but a few, and continue working, sewing and slipping off until the fringe is the length required.

The finer string is very delicate and beautiful for this fringe. Care should be taken that the work is not tight on the ruler; if it is, the child will not be able to pass the needle through the edge, and the trouble in pushing it off, instead of slipping it off, spoils the gloss and whole appearance. Many fancy things can be decorated with this fringe.

VIII. HEXAGONAL RING MAT.

This mat is also made of brass rings and is worked in two colours, tan and blue strings.

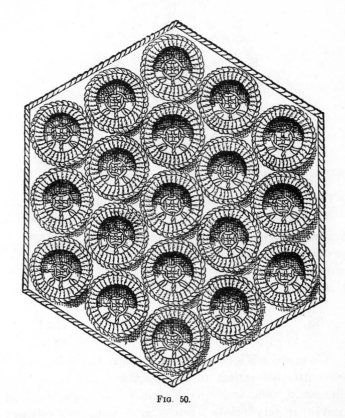

Fig. 50.

Nineteen rings are required to form the mat, and these are so arranged, that round a central ring (tan) are fastened six blue to form a hexagon, which can then be increased to any size. How this is done is best seen from the illustration (Fig. 50).

Centre.—The centre is first filled in with two double cross strands running across the centre at right angles, as in diagram of photo frame (Fig. 46).

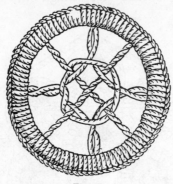

FIG. 51.

The strands are woven over and under, and caught at the quarters to the under side of the ring edge, which is best understood from diagram (Fig. 51). A tapestry needle and macramé thread is used for filling in the centre. The mat may be mounted or lined, or used as it is for a table mat.

IX.　SINGLE BUTTON-HOLE RIGHT AND LEFT (GENOESE BAR).　(SEE FIG. 43 c, PAGE 64.)

This exercise is a combination of I. and II. It comprises one button-hole stitch to the right and one to the left alternately, thus making both hands work equally. The exercise is very pretty when worked with two coloured strings.

Tie the two strings right and left at the top of foundation cords and knot in the short ends; pink and green are pretty colours together. Work one pink stitch to the right and one green stitch to the left alternately.

Four strings are required for this cord, but with the frame arranged with fixed foundations the child will only deal with the two working strings. Keep the button-hole edges firm, regular, and even.

Joining on a new string.—When joining on a new string, always tie the new string over the old end, and then knot over *both* ends for a few stitches until the beginning is firm and the ends are concealed. If the join is worked neatly it should not be noticeable.

X. CORD LACE OR GIMP.

Materials required.—1. Coarse macramé cord for foundation.

2. Macramé string No. 4 for knotting.

Method.—The quick children who are proficient in the single and double Genoese bars might be kept well employed in making cord gimp or lace. Tie the coarse cord round the width of desk in front of child and secure with a slip knot. Let the child begin to work from the knot downwards towards itself, and when necessary move the cord round the desk until the whole is knotted.

These long cords may then be used as centres for mats, or for outlining the edges of pockets or tidies. The cords and gimps form useful trimmings for the decoration and ornamentation of mats, wall-pockets, fancy tablecloths, and other miscellaneous purposes, or they may be used for braiding and manipulated into a number of designs by twisting the cords into a series of loops or rings to form monograms, etc., as in illustration.

The illustration shows a cord looped into a design and the centre filled in similar to the brass ring work. Let the children invent their own patterns, and with small pins keep them in position until sewn together with tapestry needle and twine.

The pattern shown is very simple; a child is trained to exercise its power of measurement in making the loops of equal size. When the cord is pinned accurately in equal loops the crossings must be sewn on the wrong side, and the centre crossed and recrossed to form a web. First the loop is crossed from point to base, the needle slipped on the under side to the horizontal half and crossed, after which the corners are crossed. Every crossing should pass through the exact centre of loop, and

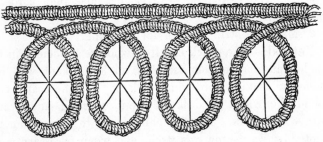

Fig. 52.

a few stitches worked to keep the eight strands together. Fine macramé twine is used for the crossing, and the cords made in this fine string are very pretty for trimming small articles, upon which the other would look too coarse.

The coarse make of macramé string forms a good foundation for large cords, and the No. 4 for gimps of finer make.

The cord can be made wide or narrow according to the foundation used.

XI. CORD AND CANE BASKET.

Another way of using up the long cords worked by the children is to insert them in the basket weaving, where they look equally as well as green plait, and brighten up the look of cane work considerably. An easy method of making a hand-basket in which a large class can be employed at the work is the following :

Method.—1. Take two slate frames of the same size and tie them tightly together. The sides of a shallow wooden box will do better, if sufficient can be obtained for the class.

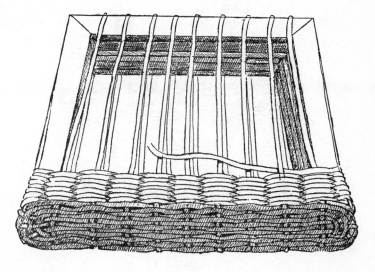

Fig. 53.

2. Soak a coarse cane (**No.** 4) and knot three lengths together.

3. Begin by tying one end round the *width* of the

slate, and button-hole strands of cane round the frame
1 inch apart down the entire length of the sides.

When the slate is full the end of cane will be at the
top. Take this end and pass down round the outer
edges of slate frame to form strands for the sides of
basket. When passing across the lower edge of slate,
weave the cane over and under the strands already there
to the other side.

FIG. 54.

Twist the cane securely at the top and return down the
sides and across the bottom again. Repeat this crossing
four times, which will give a nicely woven bottom to the
basket, and four strands up each side.

The woven piece at bottom must now be treated like the centre of an oval dinner mat, and woven round and round till the bottom edge of frame is covered. When this is done the weaving still continues round and round but proceeds up the sides. About every twelve rows a length of knotted cord is woven in and kept flat. The ends are kept inside the basket and afterwards sewn together. The four strands on right and left edges are separated and opened out in the weaving to form straight sides about 2 or 3 inches wide.

After the bottom is finished a child may proceed with the weaving unaided until the slates are covered in weaving and cords.

Finishing off.—When the weaving is complete the slates are removed by cutting the strands along the top. These strands are too short to form a border, and therefore each is pushed down close into the weaving and a new strand inserted by its side, long enough to reach to the bottom of basket and also to make a handsome interlaced border.

Pattern of top.—The new strands must measure quite 12 or 14 inches long, and a wooden or steel knitting pin will be needed to push them into place.

Take any strand, pass it behind two and down by the side of the third.

Take the second strand and do the same, and as the strands pass behind the two it will be necessary to weave them in and out those already fixed to get the border firm.

Handles.—Two lengths of cord are threaded entirely round the basket on either side, and the ends joined to form loop handles.

The basket is simple for a child to weave, and the

preparation made at first is the only one which a teacher need do for the children.

XII. DOUBLE GENOESE BAR, OR DOUBLE ALTERNATE BUTTON-HOLE STITCH. (See Fig. 43 *d*, page 64.)

This exercise is the same as preceding one, only that two stitches are worked alternately instead of one, and is therefore known as the double Genoese bar. Further exercises of this bar of three, four, five, and six stitches may be worked alternately with good effect.

Supplementary exercises for this stitch may be made upon any wire articles, such as the penny copper wire flower baskets, gridirons, toast racks, etc.,

XIII. GRIDIRON LETTER RACK.

The penny gridiron is an easy article for a child to manage, and if worked or covered with any of the foregoing patterns, may be constructed into a very pretty letter rack or wall pocket to contain a small silk duster for the drawing room. As the Genoese knot is close there will be no need to first cover the iron, as the knotting will entirely cover it.

Begin at the lower end of the handle and tie on a string of peacock blue to the right and one of yellow to the left. Simply tie on each string with a single tie knot, and leave an end which must be worked in and covered with the knotting. The small twist of tin which holds the parts together must be removed, and then the child can proceed round the whole length of the bent iron without interruption, or need of help. For long, continuous work such as this it is best to give the child

two small balls of string (in little bags) to work with
and prevent frequent joining. The alternate stitches of

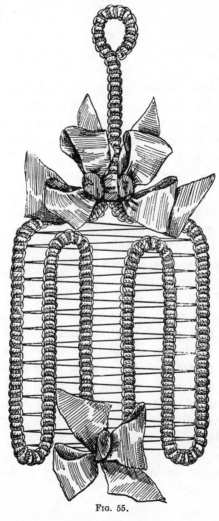

Fig. 55.

blue and yellow are very effective and is worked completely to the top loop of the handle. Here the child will have as it were to thread the stitches through the small space.

When the gridiron is entirely knotted, then a back is made by interlacing the strings across from one side to the other, producing a zig-zag pattern. For the interlacing a tapestry needle and fine macramé thread of peacock blue are used. Fasten the thread on where the knotting was begun, and with a few neat stitches join the beginning to the knotting on the handle, and then with same length of string pass the needle down through the third stitch on right and up through the third stitch on left. Continue across and *down* through the next third stitch on right, and *up* through the next third stitch on left, and so continue till the whole of the back is crossed.

The two top curves should be pulled outwards when the child is lacing across the back. When the thread is used up, simply knot a new thread to the last, and cut off the ends close, and the join will not be noticed. To finish the gridiron as a letter rack, pull the middle bars slightly forward and decorate the same with a bow of ribbon, and add another at the handle.

If a wall duster pocket is needed, make a pretty sateen or silk bag and gather the top with a full edging. Drop the bag between the front and back of the gridiron and sew the gathered edge to the top of the bars in front and to the straight top and sides of the back. Ornament with ribbon bows as before, and if the interlacing is liked, the spaces in front can be filled in, in the same way as the back.

XIV. A MUSIC OR NEWSPAPER STAND.

This very useful article is made of three old slate frames and knotted brass rings, and will provide capital employment for a large class of sixty children. The three slate frames must be of the same size, those used

Fig. 56.

in illustration are 9 × 6. The rings are medium sized curtain rings at 1s. 9d. the gross, and each slate takes twenty-four rings for the centre.

Slate frames.—Any of the flat button-hole cords are suitable, and as the stitches lie close to each other the slate can be knotted just as it is, but if the Solomon's knot be worked then the slate must be overwound with ribbon, because the colour will show through between the stitches. A colour in harmony or good contrast with the strings should be chosen.

The Genoese bar or right and left button-hole stitch in two colours is the one chosen, and the two colours are pale yellow and dark heliotrope, which go well together. Three children are employed in knotting the slate frames, and if careful in their work both sides will be exactly alike. Take care of the work to keep it fresh, and let it be put away in a large envelope after each lesson. Directly the gloss is rubbed off the string its beauty is gone. Children are always careful if their teacher is careful. Give a small ball of string of each colour, sufficient to knot a good part of the frame without a join. Joins come at the corners best. Make a tiny calico bag for each ball with a tight drawing string, and let the child work with a ball in each hand as it knots right and left round the slate. The calico bag will take all the heat of the hand and keep the string untouched and glossy. It is very disheartening to see good knotting all spoilt just for the want of a little thought and care on the part of the teacher.

The rings.—These are also knotted in single button-hole stitch. An end of a few inches is left when beginning, and knotted to the end at the finish. The rings are worked in two colours, heliotrope, and pale yellow, and arranged in rows of each. The teacher or an older girl should join them together just close to the button-hole edge with needle and macramé twine of the same

colour. When the oblong piece is ready it is sewn to
the inner edge of the frame to the button-hole edge.
Each of the slates is finished in the same way, and if
tidiness and care have been observed the two sides will
be equally good and need no lining. The rings are crossed
with eight strands to form a spider's web, and caught
together in the centre. If the ring is heliotrope then
cross it in yellow macramé twine, and *vice versâ*.

Foundation.—A piece of plain board the same size as
the slates makes the foundation, and may be covered in
leather paper or painted. To this the slates are fixed in
an upright position.

Handle.—A small cane soaked in hot water and then
bent to shape, or a child's hoop cut in half and en
amelled or knotted forms the handle.

Feet or Legs.—These are four long silk twist reels, which
any draper will gladly give away. Small spinning tops
look very well as feet. Either of the two must be enamelled like the foundation handle. The boys will delight in this painting business under the charge of a
monitress. When all is ready get a carpenter to put it
together firmly, he has means and devices and tools at
hand which the amateur carpenter has not, and it is
a pity to spoil the children's work at the end with
clumsy fixing.

At the corners the string does not entirely cover, so
a frayed rosette, or a worked ring, or a bow of ribbon
must be put as a finish.

Use.—The ends are open, and the spaces will be found
useful for papers or music. If a teacher does the fixing
herself she should fix with small screws two corner plates
to one side of each slate before the knotting is commenced.
The plates meant are like a small corner, one side of

which will fix to the slate and the other to the foundation. The one fixed to the slate will stand upright and
be covered with knotting, so that only the two holes of
the half fixed to the foundation will show.

XV. A LILY.

The petals and leaves of flowers are prettily imitated
in knotting over ribbon wire. Large flowers such as
tulips and lilies with but few petals are the best to
copy, but smaller ones can be made of finer wire and
string on the same principle. The knotting can be turned
to any shape when finished.

We will suppose a tiger lily is to be imitated ; if possible
have a real specimen to show the children, or failing
that, a good coloured picture of the flower. Pull off the
petals one by one, and count them (six) and note their
shape, or sketch shape on blackboard.

Next draw attention to the stamens, and interest children
in the flower by telling them they are going to make
one as nearly like the real one as possible with their
strings. Question upon the colour and choose strings as
near the shade as can be procured.

Materials required.—1. Yellow satin-covered ribbon
wire.

2. Two shades of pale yellow strings.

3. Yellow macramé twine and tapestry needle.

Cut the wire into lengths of 14 inches, and distribute one wire to each child. Tie on the end one
string of pale and one of dark yellow, and let the children reproduce (Ex. III. on slate), making one button-hole
stitch of each alternately till the wire is covered.

See that the work is kept flat and untwisted, and
bring the two ends together and shape into the form of

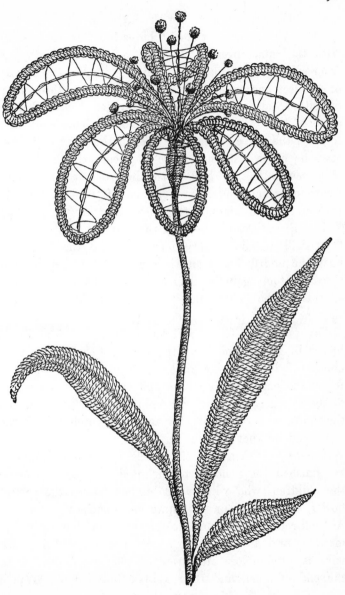

Fig. 57.

a leaf. Overwind the ends with thread or what is known
as No. 10 macramé twine. Thread a tapestry needle
with the same thread and begin to work across the leaf
from side to side, like the gridiron. Begin at the base
of the leaf and take the inner loop of every third stitch
on either side, making a zig-zag ladder from bottom to
apex of leaf. The stitches must not be pulled too tight
to affect the shape of the leaf. When the apex is reached
sew one or two stitches there to secure the ladder and
then return to the base with the same thread, thus :
weave over and under every strand of the ladder to the
base and return again to the apex, reversing the weaving.
This centre thread represents the midrib, and if pulled
tight will impart a very nice shape to the leaf. To
keep the midrib intact and in centre of leaf, return from
apex to stem again by oversewing it between every two
strands of the ladder and fasten off at the ends, when
the one leaf or petal is complete.

The Stamens. — Give out twelve pieces of string 6
inches in length and of both shades of yellow, and let
children make a double knot at one end. Into the knot
insert the end of a fine wire, and twist down the length
of the string. The wire will keep the stamens erect, and
the knot will represent the anther of each. Fray the
short end of knot with a pin.

Mounting. — When the six petals and twelve stamens
are finished they should be mounted upon a stem *before*
the children, who will be all anxiety to see the perfect
flower, and endeavour to imitate one themselves at home.
A small round stick would do for the stem, but to give a
more natural and drooping appearance a doubled coarse
wire is preferable. First tie the cluster of stamens to
the end of stem, and then a little lower down arrange

the petals. Both stamens and petals are best secured by winding round tightly with carpet thread, and when all is in position let a child overwind the whole in fine green string. The bulky part where the petals were attached will, if nicely managed, look like a good calyx, and if desired large leaves may be attached at intervals down the stem, directions for which are given in next lesson.

XVI. LEAVES.

Materials required.—1. Ribbon wire.

2. Various shades of green string or twine.

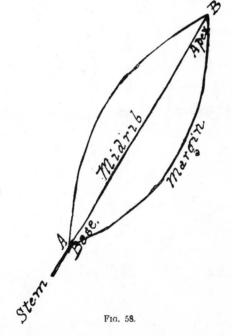

FIG. 58.

Before teaching the children how to make a leaf, it is desirable that they should previously have had a lesson upon "leaves," and be thus well acquainted with the parts, colour, growth, etc.   Question the children upon the shape and parts of a leaf, and sketch outline of one upon the blackboard, and as each part is named by the children, mark in the same upon sketch, and tell them they are about to imitate a leaf in this lesson.

Method.—Distribute to the class lengths of ribbon wire about 4 or 5 inches long.   The children have to bend the wire to the shape of blackboard sketch, which is done in the following way :

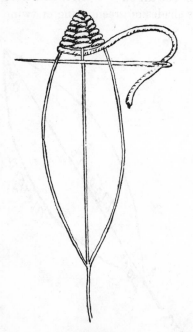

FIG. 59.

1. Bend the wire in half, and make a point at the centre.
2. Curve the sides, and bring the two ends together.
3. Twist the twine round the ends at "A," and carry it

across the centre of leaf to the apex at " B," and there sew
it over and over to the point, letting the needle pass *through*

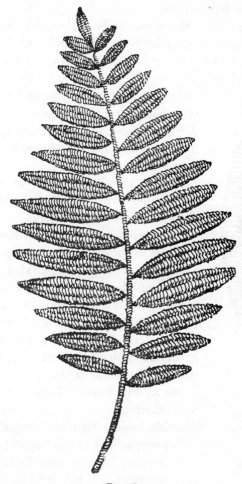

Fig. 60.

the stitches to keep it in place. For this purpose use a
tapestry needle. Lead the children to see that this central

strand represents the midrib. The leaf is filled in by weaving to and fro a long length of green twine, over and under as in mat-plaiting.

Pass the needle first across *under* the central strand, and return by passing it under both wires and *over* the centre (as in illustration). In this way the substance and margin of the leaf are represented. The weaving must be pulled close and tight, but not to such an extent that the shape of the leaf becomes affected. A teacher must use her own judgment in imitating the size and shape of different leaves.

A piece of wire is added to form the stalk, unless when shaping the leaf sufficient is allowed for the stem.

Pretty sprays of leaves and flowers can be made as shown in previous lesson. If a fern spray is to be imitated, all the leaves must be made separately, and then mounted upon a large stalk of coarse wire and covered in a winding of deep green string. The fern leaves should be made in different shades of green, graduating from a pale colour at the apex to a dark shade at the base. These sprays look well mounted on the children's cane-weaving, besides forming a valuable educative supplement to the Object Lessons.

Fig. 61.

If the leaf be large and the string will not keep tight, it is better for the children to button-hole the string each time to the wires in preference to weaving, because the strings will then keep in place without trouble.

Other flowers such as tulips, fuchsias, geraniums and other large flowers may easily be imitated. For small petals the macramé thread must be used.

Buds may be worked over small egg-shaped balls or foundations like the tennis ball (page 124) and then attached to a wire stem overwound in green thread.

XVII.   WAVED BAR OR SHELL PATTERN.
(See Fig. 43 *e*, PAGE 65.)

This bar is an exercise based upon the button-hole stitch. It somewhat resembles the corrugated appearance and shape of a cockle or scallop shell, and for that reason and because of the information and interest which could be imparted about shell-fish, that name was applied for school purposes, otherwise it is known as the " waved bar."

It is taught here upon a fixed foundation, but when the foundation strands are held the bar can be made to wave as much as desired by pushing up the stitches quite close on the foundation strands.

Stitch.—Four strings are required for the knot, the second and third strings are held tightly in the hand or fixed whilst the first and fourth take it in turns to knot across them.

Give two colours to each child : fawn and green strings look well together and may be compared to the green sea and the colour of the sand and shell on the sea shore.

Knot both on at the top of slate right and left respectively.

1. Work *seven* button-hole stitches with the right string (green).

2. Then work *seven* button-hole stitches with the left (fawn).

Push the stitches on the foundation close together, and spread out the button-hole edge to represent the edge of the shell.

Repeat 1 and 2 alternately and the pattern will be a series of waves or shells joined by a loop on either side of the exercise.

XVIII.   A ROPE FRAME.

The smallest sized Manilla rope may be used as foundations for some of the exercises, and most artistic little things can be made with it.   It may be used to decorate small tables, or inserted in the basket weaving, or arranged into handsome braided designs upon boards which may be utilized for music stands or newspaper holders.   The medium and larger sizes may be used for bell pulls, curtain bands, and fraying.

The simple frame here illustrated is only suitable for fixing to a mounted picture such as a large photograph or print.

Measure the sides of the picture and cut four pieces of rope to correspond in length.   Strain the rope tightly over the desk by tying the ends with strings to the desk underneath, and then let the children knot over the rope in two colours.   The knot used in illustration is the Shell pattern, but any of the preceding exercises are suitable.

Shell pattern.—Seven button-hole stitches right and left alternately in two coloured strings.

Begin to knot about 2 inches from the end of each piece and leave 2 inches of the strings also, knot the rope till within 2 inches of the other end and again leave two ends of string.

When all four pieces are knotted in this manner, tie

the ends very tightly with thread and then fray out the
strings and rope to form a pretty tassel at either end.
This done cross the ends, overwind tightly in string and

Fig. 62.

cover each corner with a bow of ribbon to harmonize
with the colour of the string.

XIX. BANNISTER OR TWISTED BAR.
(See Fig. 43*f*, page 65.)

This knot is most ornamental and effective; it requires four strings, the two centre threads of which form the foundation on which the knot is worked, but as these are fixed for the child, it will have to work only with the first and fourth.

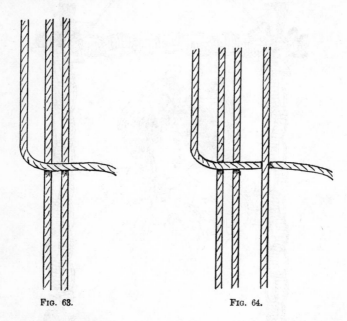

Fig. 63.   Fig. 64.

1. Take first string and pass it over the foundation strings (Fig. 63).

2. Bring fourth string down and over the end of the first (Fig. 64).

3. Thread the end of number four string across underneath the foundation and up through the loop made by the first (Fig. 65).

It will be found that the pattern twists on itself, and to make this twist regular the right string should be

Fɪɢ. 65.

passed under the foundation cords at every fifth stitch. The left-hand string is always the one placed across every time.   The bar can be worked to any length.

XX.   LETTER RACK.

This little rack is a useful and easy supplementary lesson for the quick workers of the twisted bannister bar.

It is knotted in two coloured strings, brown and pale yellow, but any other combinations might be used.   The sides are formed of two rings of 4 inches diameter, and these are looped across each other to form an ellipse in the centre.   If two rings of this size are not obtainable, let the children work a bar upon thick milliners' wire measuring 12 inches in length.   This plan will answer equally well, if not better, and can be shaped into a circle when finished, and the join hidden with a bow of ribbon. Four rings or bars must be worked for the two sides.

The handle measures 16 inches in length, and is made of a firm, coarse wire covered with Solomon knots. It

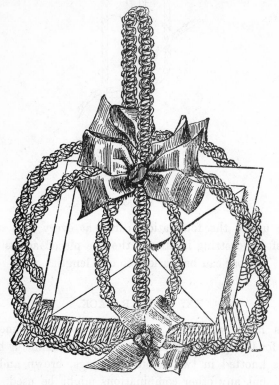

Fig. 66.

is fixed to the base and the ends bent underneath. The sides are added afterwards and fastened to the handle where the bows of ribbon hide the stitches.

The base is a stout strip of cardboard 6 inches by

2 inches. It is covered with velveteen, and then knotted across with the Genoese knot, which completely covers it. The under side is made neat with a strip of leather paper.

Bows of ribbon in harmony with the colours are added at the sides as a finish, and to hide the stitches of joining. The whole article may be made for sixpence, and less if odd dressmakers' cuttings are obtained at a cheap rate.

XXI. SOLOMON'S KNOT. (See FIG. 43 *g*, PAGE 65.)

This is a very useful and handsome knot, and is largely used in macramé lace to form a heading or centre of a star or diamond, and when tied together makes an effective open knotting pattern. It requires four strings, and is made similar to the twisted or Bannister bar; in fact, the first half of the knot is precisely the same, but the second part of the knot works back from the right-hand side. Though this knot may look intricate it is not so, but is easily learnt by the children and much liked by them. It is best to teach the knot step by step so that the children quite grasp the knot. After having learnt the previous knot, "Bannister" (Fig. 43 *f*, page 65), there will be no difficulty in working this one correctly at once, because the two are nearly alike. In the "Bannister" the left thread crosses the foundation every time, but in the "Solomon" the right and left take it in turns to cross.

1. The foundation strands are fixed, otherwise they would be the second and third strings and be held in the hand in making a lace off the slate.

2. Take left string (Fig. 67) and place across the foundation strings.

3. Take right string, place vertically down and over the end of first string.

4. Thread the end of right string across underneath the foundation strings and out through the loop made by the first string; pull both ends tightly. This completes the first half of knot which is the "Bannister" knot.

5. Take right-hand string (Fig. 68) and place across the foundation strings, the reverse of Fig. 67.

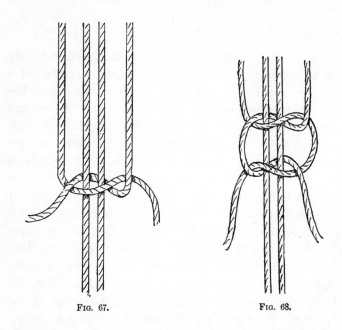

FIG. 67.   FIG. 68.

6. Bring the left string down over the end and cross under the foundation strings and up through the loop made by the right. Pull tightly and the knot is complete. Three crossings should be worked to show a single and complete knot. The knot is best taught with two coloured strings at first, and in fact always, because the combination is so very pretty and easy to understand.

The children will soon see that the left string which starts is the right to come back again, and therefore there will be a crossing of one colour throughout the work and edge of another, or the strings may be used alternately for each double crossing and produce both kinds of stitches.

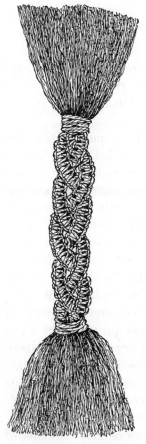

FIG. 69.—Rope Dusting-Brush.

XXII. ROPE BELL-PULL.

Cut three lengths of fine Manilla rope so that they will reach from the ceiling to within a few inches of the floor. Strain them tightly across the desk and let children knot over them from top to bottom in two coloured strings. Any of the alternate button-hole exercises or Solomon's knot are very suitable, as the knotting completely covers the rope. When the three lengths are finished plait them loosely in three and tie the ends together. The lower end is tied about 8 inches from the bottom and unravelled to form a tassel.

XXIII. ROPE DUSTING-BRUSH.

This brush is made very similar to the preceding exercise. The three pieces of small Manilla rope are 9 inches long and knotted 2 inches from either end. The three pieces are knotted with the

Solomon knot (see Fig. 43 *g*, p. 65), and when finished **are** tied tightly together at one end and plaited in three, and then again tied. Both ends are brought together, wound round and round with string, and finished with a bow of ribbon. The ends are frayed and combed like the brush in Stage I. (Fig. 25).

XXIV.   ROPE DOOR-MATS.

These mats may be made any size and would form a most useful occupation for boys if carried out on a large scale for household purposes. To give the principle of the work a small door-mat for a doll's house is here described.

Cut the rope into 6-inch lengths, and on the first rope tie *four* macramé strings thus : Let the strings be red, and each 1 yard long. Double each string in half and tie one to the rope 1 inch from either end, and the other two at equal distances in the middle. The two ends of each string are used for tying on the other ropes. Place the second piece of rope between the strings of all four sets and then tie this rope to the first one. A single tie knot is all that is necessary until the *last* rope is tied on, and then the knot must be double. The ropes should be added until the mat measures a square or oblong. The knotting should be kept quite straight across the mat, and it should have the appearance of four narrow red stripes running across it. The inch ends on either side are now to be ravelled or frayed out and cut quite even, and the mat is finished. If the rope be stout, double strings should be used as in illustration.

Upon this same plan whole straws may be knotted together to make photo frames, table mats, washstand splashers and a variety of useful things, in fact, if wooden moulds of hats and baskets are to be had, the straws can be tied to any shape in the same way as the Swiss tie the straw hats now seen in this country.

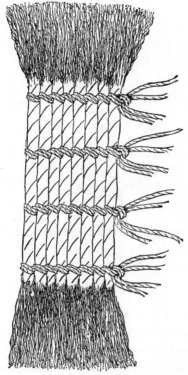

Fig. 70.

The straws are a little larger at one end than the other, therefore when joining, always insert the small end of one straw into the large end of the other, and continue tying as if all in one piece. Coloured straws interspersed with white are very effective for frames and

splashers or window blinds, and the ends may be vandyked
or bound as desired.

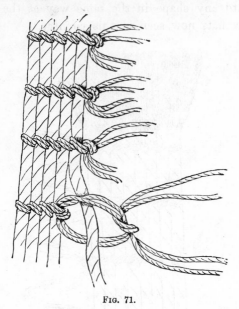

Fig. 71.

XXV.   CORD DINNER-MATS.

These mats are also knotted upon the same principle
as the others but are worked round instead of straight
across.   All the strings must be knotted to the end of the
cord which will form the centre of mat and one pair must be
tied right and left alternately for the first 4 inches of the
cord.   Stiff blind cord or small rope is best for the work
and No. 4 macramé string.   Arrange the strings that
they radiate round pretty evenly, but a little closer
together at the ends.   The cord is laid flat between the
strings and knotted round and round until the mat is
the size required.   Large door-mats knotted of rope and

string may be made in this manner, but the occupation is only fit for big strong boys.

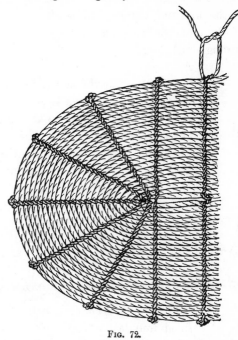

FIG. 72.

XXVI. SINGLE TATTED BAR.
(SEE FIG. 43 *h*, PAGE 65.)

The tatted knot is a very pretty stitch, it is worked with one string upon a foundation string or strings, according to the size of the bar required. The working string needs to be long as all the work is made by it and it soon gets used up.

The stitch or knot is very like two button-hole stitches reversed to each other and is made on that principle.

The foundation string is held or fixed in the right

hand and the knot is made with the left. It can be worked from the right also.

1. Take the knotting thread and work one button-hole stitch over the foundation in the ordinary way, *over*, *under*, and *up* through the loop. Draw it up tightly but not too tight.

2. Take the thread again and work a second stitch the reverse way, viz.: *under*, then *over* the foundation and *down* through the loop made by itself. This makes the knot and differs from the entire button-hole stitch by the knot looking separate and joined together by a cross-bar. It is quickly understood by the children.

XXVII.   DOUBLE TATTED BAR.

Four strings are needed for this exercise. It is worked exactly like the Single Tatted Bar of two strings, but with alternate knots right and left. Upon the fixed foundation cords tie two different coloured strings (blue and pink).

1. Take the blue string and make a tatted knot upon the foundation cords to the right, thus : *over*, *under*, and *up* through the loop, and then *under*, *over*, and *down* through the loop, which completes the two parts of the knot.

Fig. 73.

2. Take the pink string and work a tatted knot to the left in the same way—*over*, *under*, and *up* through the loop, then *under*, *over*, and *down* through the loop.

Repeat alternate knots right and left. The cord has a pretty double flat edge composed of a small loop and crossbar.

XXVIII. SINGLE AND DOUBLE LOOP FRINGES.

From the previous exercises of single and double tatted bars may be made single and double loop fringes.

The plan is very simple, as no alteration is needed in working the stitch. The loop is made at a certain distance down the foundation cord and then pushed up, when the length of the string left unknotted stands out as a loop.

The equal distance or space left between the stitches is obtained by inserting a strip of wood or cardboard each time a stitch is made, and when the complete knot is finished, the strip of wood or cardboard is pulled out and the stitch pushed up, and a series of regular loops are thus formed. The size of the loop depends upon the width of the wood or cardboard strip inserted. The single fringe is useful for the borders of mats or edges of pockets.

The double tatted bar, worked with two coloured strings, makes an effective double looped fringe. The loops are made

Fig. 74.

right and left alternately in the same manner as a single fringe. Long strips of these double loops, joined together, make very pretty antimacassars. The loops are interlaced to join the strips together. Take a bone crochet-hook and pull the first loop of one strip through the first loop of the second strip. Then pull second loop of first strip through that to make a new loop, and so interlace right and left till the whole strip is joined together.

This exercise is very simple for a child to do, as there is no actual crochet work, but only drawing the loops in and out each other. Little fingers could interlace large loops without the use of a crochet needle.

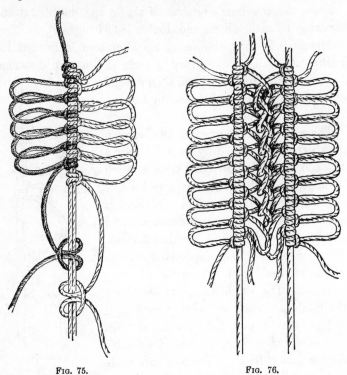

Fig. 75.　　　　　　Fig. 76.

A very pretty crossing of the two colours down the whole length of the strips adds much to the beauty of the work. The appearance is similar to the joining of hairpin crochet work on page 245.

XXIX. SINGLE AND DOUBLE LOOP ROSETTES.

Single loop rosette.—The children can work a certain number of loops and draw them up on the foundation string to form a ring or rosette.

A strip of cardboard, 1½ inches wide, will keep the stitches that distance apart and make loops ¾ inch deep. The size of the loop will be either large or small according to the width of the strip inserted. The rosettes may be crocheted together to form doyleys, or used as blossoms of flowers. Long strips of single loop fringes are useful for the borders of table-mats. Give the children a card on which to mount their flowers and twist the strings for the stem. Sew the flower and stem to a card with needle and cotton.

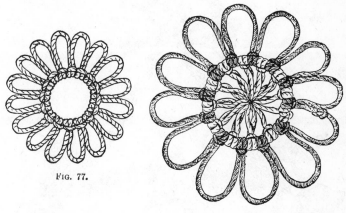

Fig. 77.

Fig. 78.

Double loop rosettes.—Let the children work a long strip of double loop fringe and then thread a string through one set of loops, and draw up tightly.

Join the first and last strings to form another loop on the outer circle. These rosettes may be joined together to form strips for antimacassars, or be joined in rounds, hexagons, or squares to make doyleys. A fringe may be added to these by casting on short strings in the loops and fraying out the ends.

If the drawn part be pulled downwards it resembles the cup of a flower, and if a stem of wire be attached, a few rosettes might be utilized as such and mounted with leaves, and the stem over-wound in fine green twine, as illustrated in "Toilet Tidy."

XXX. A TOILET TIDY.

This little pocket can be made any size and of any shape. The one in illustration is made of two pieces

FIG. 79.

of cardboard, back and front. The pocket may be covered in crinkled paper or sateen lining or silk or velveteen, and then decorated with knotting as seen in illustration. The edge is trimmed with a cord of single chain knot (Ex. XLI.).

The front of pocket is ornamented with small leaves (Ex. XVI.) and tatted flowers (Ex. XXIX.). The same decoration may be carried out on any pockets, mats, or tidies.

XXXI. A ROUND TABLE MAT.

The round mat in illustration measures 8 inches in diameter. The foundation is of stout cardboard and

FIG. 80.

the centre is made of a knotted cord wound in spiral fashion till the mat is nearly full. Any of the round knotted cords of Stage I., or the flat foundation cords of Stage II. are suitable. These centres will be found a very effectual way of using up the long cords worked by the quick children in Stages I. and II.

The fringe is made as described under tatted looped fringe, and this is sewn round four times on the edge of the mat. If the cardboard is soft for working, a child of seven can sew the centre cord round and round till mat is full. The underside of mat is made neat with a circle of leather paper to hide the stitches.

NETTING.

Simple netting with string is a splendid occupation for boys. They soon learn the ONE stitch, and are then quite independent to continue their work without further help from the teacher. The materials are inexpensive and simple, and the work is strong, durable, and useful. One great advantage of the occupation is that it never comes undone, or gets out of order like knitting and crochet, because every stitch is independent and knotted securely.

Cabbage, fishing, potato nets, and ladies' shopping bags are articles easily made by the boys, and the most expert might try curtains, hammocks, and lawn tennis nets. For beginners the ordinary shop string is quite good enough and will make common bags, nets, etc.

The netting meshes and needles most useful for the children are wooden ones about an inch wide, and sold at tenpence per dozen.

The size of the stitch or loop depends upon the width of the mesh. The needle must not be too large or it will be difficult to push through the loop, and yet if too small it will hold but a small quantity of string. As a child becomes advanced in the work a steel mesh and fine string or twine could be substituted.

The work might be utilized as an occupation for girls after the boys have netted the foundation, because plain netting admits of being much improved by darning, or, as better known to the children, of being woven in and out the holes with a needle and thread so as to produce a pattern of squares, diamonds, stripes, or any geometrical figure. Show children the implements and illustrate the use of each before attempting to teach the stitch.

To fill the netting mesh thread the end of string through the hole in shank, tie it and then pass the string through the prongs from end to end until moderately full. If fine loops are being worked then a long steel needle should be used. Crochet and knitting cotton are both suitable for fine netting and for darning.

The work requires a firm foundation, and for this purpose the iron supports of the desk are valuable to enable the "stirrup" or foundation cord to be attached, and allow of the resistance so necessary when tightening the knot.

The "stirrup" should be of the stout macramé cord. Give each child 1 yard of this cord to form the "stirrup." Knot the two ends together and fasten the loop to some convenient corner or iron work of the desk so that the child gets the "stirrup" in front of him ready for learning the netting stitch.

Netting stitch.—The mesh is held horizontally in the left hand and the needle in the right. Begin by tying the end of string on needle to the string of "stirrup." See that the "stirrup" is not too long and that the child gets a firm pull of it.

Position of hands.—1. Take the mesh in left hand and hold it firmly between the thumb and first finger, the thumb to be uppermost, and bring the string over it and hold the mesh under the string and close to the knot just tied.

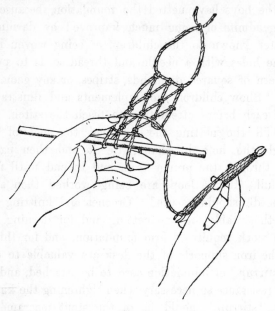

FIG. 81.

2. Take the needle in the right hand and bring the thread down from the knot, over the mesh and over the front of the left hand and then round to the back, enclosing the third and second fingers of left hand in a loop. Pass the thread from behind the mesh across to the thumb and hold it there by pressure. Illustrate on blackboard the course of the thread and compare it to the making of the figure " 8." This part must be made clear before the knot is taken. Several exercises

of taking up the implements and holding in position
and "throwing the thread" might be done for one lesson.
If a large demonstration sheet of Fig. 81 be placed in
front of the class it will save the teacher much time
and trouble because, although the knot may be demonstrated with rope in front of class, yet there will be
some who will need individual attention.

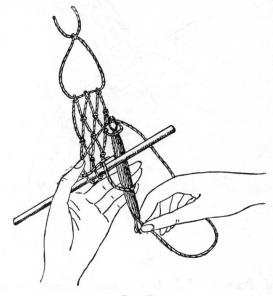

Fig. 82.

Second Position.—Carry the string loosely towards the
right *over* the loop of "stirrup," and down behind the
mesh and left hand, bringing the needle in front and
pass it *through the loop* on the second and third fingers,
under the mesh and *through the loop* of the "stirrup," and
pull out *over* the string which forms the upper loop of the
figure "8." Fig. 82 shows the position of the hands and
a few rows worked, but in the first row every stitch

would be taken through the loop of the "stirrup," and all successive rows would be worked into the loops of the previous row.

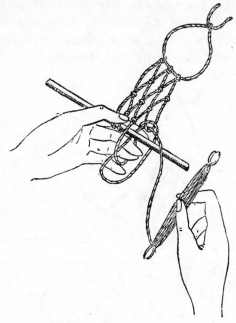

FIG. 83.

Third Position.—This is the most difficult to manage because the knot has to be tightened, and this is often very loose and uneven until the knack is known. When the hands are in "Position II.," draw the children's attention to the loops that have been formed.

Let the needle be pulled out through the "stirrup" and a loop tightened round the little finger, there will then be three separate loops to keep count of, and if special attention is not drawn to these, the children will slip all off their fingers at once and knot loose, uneven loops.

The first loop made was round the second and third fingers of left hand.

The second loop made was across under the thumb of left hand.

The third loop made was the lower one round the little finger.

Impress upon the children that these three loops must take their turn in being let go, and if all go together the knot will be made too soon and will not fit tight to the mesh.

Tightening the knot.—When the loops are clearly demonstrated, teach the knot. The needle hand must be kept tight, and drawing up all the time until the three loops are off the fingers. Hold the needle straight out and tighten the loop round the little finger, and then let go FIRST the loop held under the thumb. Keep the mesh up close to the knot while tightening, and then let go the SECOND loop on the second and third fingers. Keep pulling tight, and be careful to let the LAST loop off gradually and pull the loop tightly round the mesh until the little finger is drawn up close to it, then slip the finger out and pull the stitch sharply and tight to the mesh. Repeat the process for every stitch till there are as many stitches as are required. When the first row is done on the "stirrup," then pull out the mesh and begin again at the left-hand loopside. The working string is on the right so the work must be turned over to bring the string on the left ready for the next row.

Second row.—Place the mesh in position close up to the lower edge of the row of loops and work another set of loops as before, but this time taking every stitch into a separate loop in regular succession.

Turn the work over for every new row, because netting is always worked from left to right. When the needle is empty it must be refilled and the string knotted. If possible keep the knots at the end of the rows. Directly the boys can do the stitch let them make "something."

Note.—For teaching purposes the flat 6-inch rulers might be used as meshes, and a bodkin or blunt threader, with length of string, as a temporary needle, until the stitch is known.

XXXII.   A TENNIS NET.

Now that "Tennis" is such a popular game, it is well to tell the children of what the game consists, and let the class make a "Tennis Set."   The boys can net or

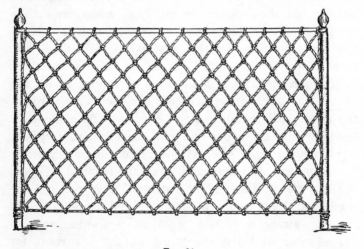

Fig. 84.

knot a miniature tennis net, and with two kindergarten sticks to represent the supports and the "stirrup" string untied and running through the top, a very good imitation of one is obtained.

XXXIII. A TENNIS RACQUET AND BALL.

The Racquet.—Another portion of the class can be employed in making racquets. Distribute pieces of coarse weaving-cane or ribbon-wire, about 16 inches long, and

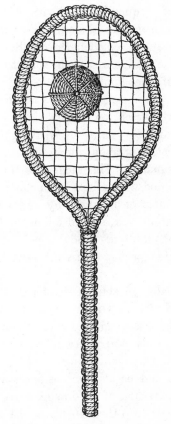

FIG. 85.

let the children knot, in two colours, any of the right and left button-hole stitches.

Begin about 4 inches from one end and knot till about

4 inches from the other, then bend the cane or wire round
into shape, and bring the two unknotted ends together for
the handle.   Tie them temporarily together and knot
over both at once to form the handle.   Finish off the
ends neatly into the knotting.

The centre of racquet is filled with crossings and interlacings of fine macramé thread.   For this part use a
tapestry needle and a long length of yellow twine.   Begin
near the handle and cross from side to side at every
fourth stitch of the knotting.   Slip the needle on the
under side of the stitches when passing the thread to
the next fourth stitch on either side.   When the top
is reached, return *downwards* by weaving the needle over
and under the cross strands, and return at equal distances
so as to form squares.   The racquet is then finished, but
may be ornamented with a bow of ribbon.   A conversation
about the lightness of it, the why and wherefore of the
lightness, the catgut, etc., should follow, and a real racquet
be shown to the children.   Make a pair of small racquets
and put a knotted pocket across the centre to form toilet
tidies.

The Ball.—Balls suitable in size for this toy racquet are
those used in Fröebel's Gift I.   Get any shabby or worn
balls from the babies' room, and cover them in string thus :
Hold the ball firmly and overwind it with eight strands
of the ordinary macramé string.   Let the strands cross
top and bottom and be at even distances apart, somewhat
resembling the division of an orange.   Sew a few stitches
top and bottom to keep them in place with tapestry needle
and macramé *thread*, and then begin to work round and
round the ball on the strings.   Use the same needle and
thread from the top, and pass the needle under a strand,
back, and under it again, and then pass to the next

strand and do the same. Continue working round the strands till the ball is covered. Dark brown string looks well for the balls. If any worn balls are not obtainable,

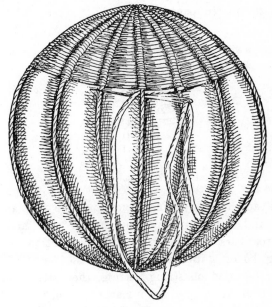

Fig. 86.

then make some balls of frayings or knitting cotton, and cover them in the same way.

To apply these little articles to a use the ball can be attached to the centre of the racquet and stuck with pins.

XXXIV. DARNING ON NETTING.

This occupation might be taken by girls with advantage, because they might do netting in knitting and crochet cottons. Some of the coloured crochet cottons are very effective and very durable, and they might net long and short window curtains, and afterwards darn them. Any geometrical figures are obtainable in the darning. A simple illustration of how it is done is given here, but numerous patterns may be worked from the drawing copies on squared paper.

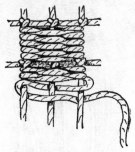

Fig. 87.

Take any two adjoining squares of the net, and with needle and thread weave the needle over and under the three bars, to and fro as in illustration. Let the darning be of a different colour to the netting. If the darning be tried on string netting, then strain the foundation over an empty slate frame, so that the darning may be kept flat and regular and easy to work.

XXXV. A KNOTTED BOX.

This is a simple way of covering any box with knotting, and is easy of preparation for the teacher, and easy and simple for the child to work. Round boxes are most suitable because there are no corners, but square boxes may be worked equally well with a little care. The box in illustration is a pound butter-box made of thin brown cardboard. A round or square collar-box may be knotted in the same way.

Preparation.—Pierce holes in the bottom all round the edge of circle and about half-an-inch apart. Do the same at the top of the rim, and let these holes be exactly above those on the bottom because the strands must be straight for working.

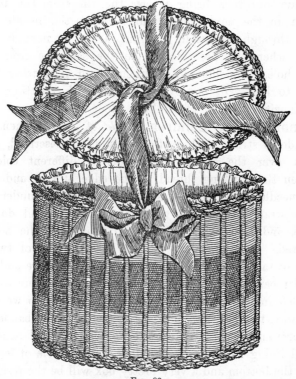

FIG. 88.

Thread a carpet needle or threader with string and work vertical strands down the side of box thus:

1. Begin with a knot, and push the needle outwards through the bottom, this brings the thread on the outside and coming from the bottom.

2. Bring it up the side, pass it *over* the rim, and from the inside push it out at the top hole *above* the under one where it first came out. The string must be uninterrupted from bottom to top for the knotting.

3. Pass the needle through the next top hole from the outside and then bring it *over* the rim from the inside down to the next bottom hole. Here the needle will pass through to inside and out again at next bottom hole, when the process will be the same as from the first hole. The horizontal stitches used in getting from hole to hole will be covered *outside* with knotting, and *inside* with a lining of crinkled paper or silk.

Knotting for Children.—*Side of Box.*—When the outside is strung with vertical strands as described, then work over the strings in rounds of different colours. Fasten the working thread to the edge of rim, and pass the needle under first strand, then back and under the same strand again. Go to the next strand and do the same, and so continue round and round till the box is covered. The sides are worked with a band of twelve rows of tan string top and bottom. To these are added a similar band of pink, and the centre portion left unworked is filled in with green. It will be found best to work in this way, top and bottom each time, so that the bands are uniform and even. Line the inside with crinkled paper or a full lining of sateen or silk, and paste a circle of leather over the bottom and a very pretty box will be the result.

Lid of Box.—The top is a plain circle without a rim. To make the box useful for trinkets or toilet accessories the lid can be worked in similar fashion. Make a hole in the centre of circle, and through this hole each time button-hole strands at even distances all round the edge, keeping the strands in a notch about half-an-inch apart.

Begin at the centre and work round and round to the edge. When finished, line the under side to match the box. The colours used in box of illustration are tan and pink and green strings, lined with pink of the same shade.

Cords.—Three children can be employed in making the knotted cords which are sewn round the top and bottom of box and to the edge of the lid.

The pattern is the Cable or Spiral Cord in Stage I., Fig. 32, knotted with two strings of green and two of pink.

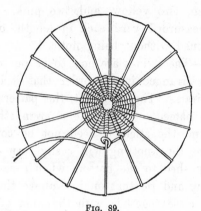

FIG. 89.

A pretty bow of green ribbon hides the hole in the top, and two strings tie the lid to the box. The box is very pretty and light to handle, and easy for small children to do.

XXXVI. A KNOTTED WHIP.

This exercise is good for covering a round foundation, such as a whip handle or a rope bell-pull. The knot is the ordinary common knot used in tying parcels and packages. The knotting assumes a spiral form as it is worked. The knots are made round and round the foundation until it is covered.   The pattern or effect can be varied by using different coloured strings, or by working so many rows in one colour and then joining on a second set, and alternating the two colours in sections throughout the length.

Boy's Whip.—The handle and thong are knotted in the same stitch.   For the handle buy a round penny blind-stick and cut into three pieces for handles, or have a piece of rope.

Select three different coloured strings, green, yellow, and pink.   Cut duplicates of each colour so that there are two green, two yellow, and two pink.   The strings need only measure 1 yard each in length, because they are easily joined without being noticed.

Pattern.—The strings are now to be put on the stick, and must be arranged in the order that it is wished to form the spirals.   Therefore, let the pattern be as the strings were named.   First take a *green* string and tie one end round the stick, it need not be commenced at the bottom as the knotting will easily turn on the stick and can be pushed to the bottom when necessary.   Take a *yellow* string and tie that on just above the green, and put the two close together with the knot of green first, and the knot of yellow coming a little to the left of it. This point is noticed here because each new string must be tied on a little to the left of the last, so that the six strings and their six knots arrange themselves quite round the stick.   Tie the first to the second thus:

The knot.—Take the right string across in the left hand, and the left string in the right, then tie one-half of a button-hole knot.   Change hands again with the strings and tie as before, when the first string should be where it was at starting, on the right.   Care must be taken that the right-hand string comes back to the right when the second tie of the knot is made, and that the second string is carried forward to become the right string for the next knot. If this point is clearly shown at first the work will be knotted correctly, because the children will notice that the strings are put back in the order they were cast on.

Tie on the third string above the yellow and bring the knot to the left of the one just tied. Tie the yellow string to the pink twice, and throw the yellow string back to the right. The other three strings are tied and knotted on in the same order, green, yellow, and pink, till the knots reach round to the first string. Here all the strings must be pushed down close together on the stick, and the first and sixth tied together. The circle is now complete and ready for the second round to be knotted. Always remember to use a string once, first as left and then as the right in each knot, and throw the right string back when finished. The knots must be kept at regular distances round the stick.

Method of holding.—The work can be done if the stick is fixed in an opening or wedged between the child and the desk. In this case the knot is made each time on the upper side of the stick and the work turned to the right after each knot. The child can also hold the stick between his knees and knot in an upright position, but the quickest way and the best is to let two children work together, by letting one hold and turn the stick whilst the other knots. They change after each one has knotted six or twelve rounds.

The work can be slipped off on to larger or smaller foundations, and upon this plan the beginning of the whip can be worked on a stick a little larger and a whistle inserted, then the handle portion can be knotted on the blind stick and the thong continued on a blind cord till long enough.

XXXVII. ROPE BELL-PULL (2).

This handsome bell-pull is knotted upon the stoutest kind of Manilla rope, sold at 3d. per yard.   It is knotted

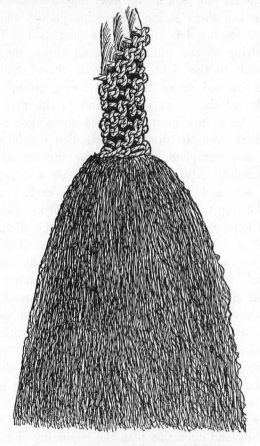

Fig. 90.

entirely in white coarse macramé string No. 2, and is worked in the same way as the rope whip.

Six strings are knotted on separately round the rope

foundation, about 6 inches from the end, and then worked in spiral fashion. The ambulance or flat knot is very suitable for this spiral knotting and will give a

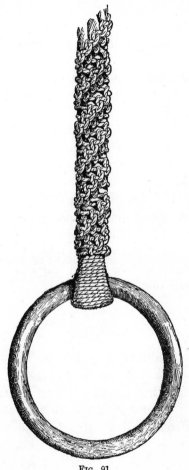

Fig. 91.

flat spiral knotting instead of raised as in the pattern illustrated. If the flat knot be used the strings should be of two colours, and tied on alternately at the commencement. Every knot will be a mixture of the two colours and joined by alternate strings of the colours. When finished the spiral effect is very good.

Handles.—Bell-pulls made on Manilla rope must have the handle end finished as a frayed tassel or bound over a wooden ring.

The ring in illustration is one of those used for ring drill and sold at sixpence each. It is a large, plainly polished ring.

The end of the rope is unplaited for 6 inches, passed over the ring, and the end tightly wound in with rows of string to meet the knotting. The ring gives a nice finish to the bell-pull.

When a child is working a large rope of this kind it is best to suspend it over a rod or gas pipe, so that the child may work walking round it. Only one or two children in a class would be employed on such work, and an ingenious teacher would quickly find ways and means of simplifying the working.

FRINGES.

Now that the children have worked through a number of different knots they should be shown how, by combining the knots already known, very pretty and useful fringes can be made. At first it is best to take the children in class form and teach all at once, because the foundation cords are now to be held by the child, and a little showing will be required for the first lesson.

The round penny blind-sticks answer admirably for a large class taking the work, because the stick can be fixed in the open iron work of the desks, or be rested in two hooks which can be screwed in at either end of the desk without interfering with any other work.

The great advantage which these sticks have over string is that two children, or even three, can knot on the same stick; that the sticks can be collected easily and laid in an umbrella box without getting into the tangled state which is inevitable with string; and then, most important of all, the sticks afford that firmness and resistance which is required when two or more children are pulling at the same thing. Stair rods are also very good, and two can be used in one desk.

The hooks are a necessity, independent of the sticks, because the children need them on which to attach their loops when knotting over a cord. The sticks or rods can be filled, and the knotting slipped off on to a thick string ready for use as a fringe.

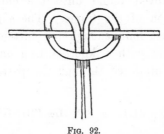

Fig. 92.

Lesson.—Suppose the class to be seated, two in a desk, and a blind stick fitted across the desk before them. Let every two children in the same desk work with the same coloured string and at the same pattern, because it will be found more interesting for the two children concerned to keep pace with each other, and afterwards, when the class will be working various patterns, the whole will be easier for the teacher to examine.

Casting on.—1. Take string, double in half. Show.

2. Pass the two ends up under the stick, and bring them over and down through the loop. Repeat for each string (Fig. 92).

After the following exercises have been worked with the children, then they should be allowed to invent patterns themselves.

The childrens' inventions can be worked on the knotting or slate frame, and the work kept in their brown paper bags as before.

The slates need not be drilled for these fringes, but a cord or two is tied tightly round the long way of the frame, and the strings knotted on these cords. Tie the cords very tightly, and let the tie be on the left-hand side of frame, because the knotting is worked from left to right. When one side of the frame is full it can be turned over, or the work moved round until the child has worked the double length of the frame. The pieces worked in this way are just long enough for curtain bands, which could be finished with a knotted ring on each end and have a ribbon interlaced through the pattern.

XXXVIII. A SINGLE FRINGE.

This fringe is made of the bannister bar stitch (Ex. XIX.). As the foundation strands are not fixed, the child must either hold them or they must be temporarily fixed to the desk or frame with a drawing pin. Either of these ways will be found good. When the knotting strings are used up as short as the foundation string, then the bar is finished and the ends must be unravelled and frayed out. In casting on the strings for Corkscrew, Bannister, Solomon, Genoese, Shell, and Tatted knots, the strings must be divided unequally. The knotting end must be four times as long as the string held for the foundation.

The insertion is worked on the same principle as the fringe. The lower ends of the strings are cut short and frayed to match the heading. The insertion may be threaded with ribbon, and rings added at each end and the strips used as curtain bands, or the strings, top and

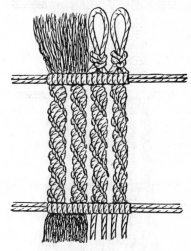

Fig. 93.

bottom, might be left long enough to tie several strips together to make an antimacassar. Ribbons should be interlaced through the strips and the ends finished to a point with a string tassel.

XXXIX. DOUBLE FRINGE (1).

This fringe consists of double Genoese and Corkscrew knots.

Casting on.—Cut the strings in 2-yard lengths, and of two colours, green and brown. Double down about a third and pass the loop down under the top cord and then

bring the two ends, one long and one short, through the
loop.   Cast on one green and one brown string all along
the cord in this way.   Each casting on gives two working
strings.   The first pattern is double Genoese knot, and

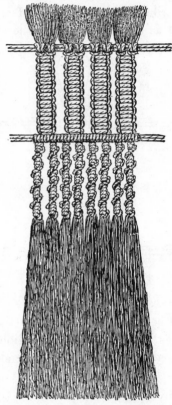

Fig. 94.

in this the right and left strings will have to be the long
ones.   See that the strings are all evenly cast on before
allowing any knotting.   The second and third strings are
the foundation strings, therefore take these and fix them

ready for working. They may be passed down underneath
the second cord, and then separately knotted on to it

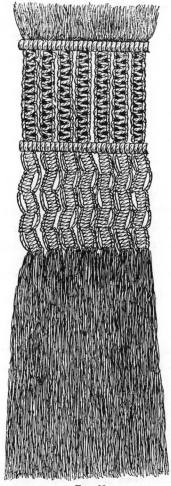

Fig. 95.

with a single button-hole stitch. Each string must make
two stitches, and should resemble two beads. When the

knotting reaches the second cord then the two working strings are knotted on in the same way. Every string thus knotted on the second cord is free and ready for a new pattern. The lower pattern is corkscrew fringe. If the next pattern also requires a long and short string, then the strings might be cast on evenly at first and changed about in the second exercise. Five twists of the corkscrew are worked upon every two strings, and the ends frayed out.

XL. DOUBLE FRINGE (2).   (Fig. 95.)

Frayed Heading.—To get this frayed heading the strings must be cast on in the following way:

Double strings and tie a loose knot on the loop end, then pass the knotted loop up under the foundation cord. (When the knotting is finished these loose knots are untied, the loop cut, and the ends frayed out.) Hold the knot in the fingers under the cord, and button-hole each string on to it with two stitches, as described for second cord.

First pattern is the Solomon's knot (Ex. XXI.). There are nine of these knots worked in two-coloured strings. The strings are then knotted on to the second cord, and a waved bar of five shells finishes the fringe (Ex. XVII.).

EXERCISES WITHOUT A FIXED FOUNDATION.

The exercises taught up to the present in Stage II. have been worked upon strings that were fixed in position or upon the firmer foundations of wire or rope, any of which foundations allowed both hands free to make the knots.

The exercises of this group, the knotting of which is similar in character to that already taught, present a new difficulty to the child, in its having to hold the foundation string while the knot is being made. The

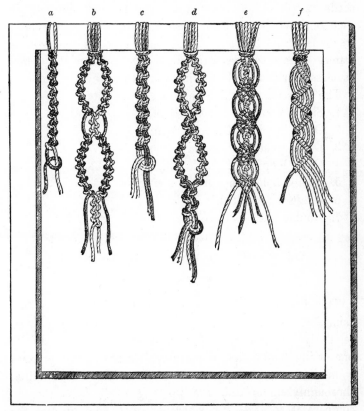

FIG. 96.—Slate, showing Exercises without a Fixed Foundation.

exercises of this group form an excellent preparation for the more advanced work of Stage III. The frame is used for the exercises and the strings fastened to the top bar. As the cords are difficult to manage if worked longer than 2 or 3 inches it is advisable to put horizontal strings across the frame at these distances, and knot the working strings on them as shown in previous exercises on fringes. These cross strands will keep the cords in place, and the child can proceed again after each one, with the same pattern, until the lower end of frame is reached, where the strings may be tied to the frame. The exercises can all be worked on the frame as class work, and shown just like the previous ones.

The exercises of this group are:
1. Single chain of see-saw knot.
2. Open looping of single chain.
3. Double chain of see-saw knot.
4. Open looping of single and double chains.
5. Button-hole gimp of six strings.
6. A zig-zag pattern.
7. Double shell pattern.

XLI.   SINGLE CHAIN OF SEE-SAW KNOT.

(SEE FIG. 96 *a*, PAGE 144.)

This is the first knot taught without a fixed foundation, and its only difficulty to young children is the tying regularly and evenly. The basis of the knot is to let one string loop round the other alternately, and produce a flat narrow vandyke cord. To make the children thoroughly understand the working of it, it is well to compare it to a see-saw where one end goes up and the other down. In this way the two hands work alternately. The hand holding the downward string must be kept perfectly straight and tight, and on no pretence whatever must it be slackened, otherwise the knot will be wrong. This is a crucial point to be attended to, but the children soon see what is required and how the knot looks when it is correctly worked.

To teach the exercise two strings of different colours are needed to enable the teacher to give definite commands.

Take two strings, a half yard in length, and knot together. Two strings of a distinct colour, such as red and white, are best for the exercise. Distribute a pair of strings to each child. The knot is slipped over the hook, or top of slate frame in front of child, and a single tie knot made to hold it in position.

1. Take the red string in the left hand and hold it perfectly straight down on the desk, and it must be impressed strongly upon the children that this hand must maintain its position and not move.

2. Take the white string in the left hand and make a single button-hole stitch upon the red string, let the stitch thus made slide upon the tight string upwards into position.

3. Change position of hands. The right-hand string is now held down and the red knotted upon it in the same way. At first the children will want to change the strings into opposite hands, but to make matters clear it is well to name the hands after the strings and call them the red hand and white hand respectively.

The cord made can be used for various purposes, such as thongs for whips, fringes, cords to ornament pockets, etc., or it may be used to make shopping bags.

The children have really learnt this exercise before on a fixed foundation, but in this case they hold a foundation string alternately with either hand. With two coloured strings the children will not mistake which one it is to knot, and the majority of the class will get the exercise

Single Chain of
See-Saw Knot.

Double Chain of
See-Saw Knot.

Open Looping of Single Chain.

FIG. 96 enlarged, showing how the

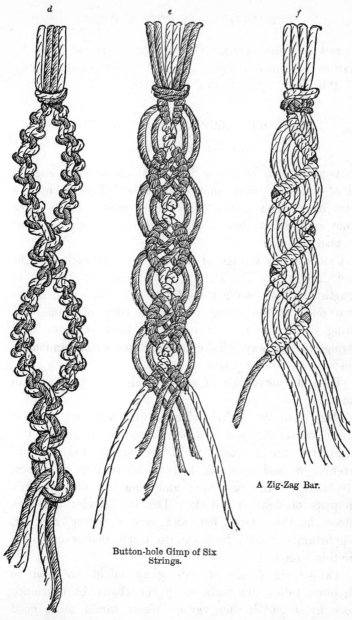

d e f

A Zig-Zag Bar.

Button-hole Gimp of Six
Strings.

Open Looping of Single
and Double Chains.

exercises are worked on Class Slate.

correct the first time. The reliable workers might be started at once to make a hand-bag composed entirely of this knot. (Ex. XLVIII. and XLIX.)

XLII. OPEN LOOPING OF SINGLE CHAIN.

(SEE FIG. 96 *b*, PAGE 144.)

A good plan to follow is to let one exercise suggest another of the same knot if possible before teaching a new one. The present exercise is made of the same knot as the last, but in this case four strings are used instead of two.

Cast on two strings of different colours such as light and dark blue. The strings should measure 2 yards in length as they soon get used up. To cast on, pass the two ends of the string under the edge of frame and bring them over down through the loop. Cast on both strings in this way. Take the first two strings and upon them work twelve chain knots.

Take the next pair of strings and work twelve chain knots.

Next take the right string of first pair and the left string of second pair and work four chain knots; this completes the exercise, which is simply the previous exercise worked according to numbers to form a pattern. Repeat from the beginning and take the strings again in pairs of light and dark. The two shades are combined in the centre bar and give a pretty contrast. Opportunity should be taken to teach shades of colour in this exercise.

Use.—Long pieces of this gimp might be used to decorate tidies and mats, or if the chains be continued to a great length then several pieces would make good

reins and thongs for whips. Insertions and fringes of this
pattern may be made worked round the slate frame as
described under Fringes.

XLIII. DOUBLE CHAIN OF SEE-SAW KNOT.
(See Fig. 96 c, page 144.)

This exercise is worked precisely in the same manner
as the single chain but with four threads instead of two.
Any equal number of strands may be used for this
stitch, so that numerous additional examples in greater
numbers may be taught if desired. The strings should
lie flat and moderately tight when using more than one
string.

XLIV. OPEN LOOPING OF SINGLE AND DOUBLE CHAINS.
(See Fig. 96 d, page 145.)

Cast on two strings of different colours, 2 yards in
length, which will give four working threads 1 yard long.
Green and pink, or blue and yellow are good combinations.

Knot twelve stitches with the first pair of strings and
twelve stitches with the second.

Take each pair in right and left hands respectively
and knot a double chain of six stitches.

Divide the strings again into pairs and work twelve
knots on each as before, and then connect with a double
chain. Repeat till strings are used up.

XLV. BUTTON-HOLE GIMP OF SIX STRINGS.
(See Fig. 96 e, page 145.)

1. Cast on one yellow string, and one heliotrope on
either side of it. There are now six working strings as
follows : two heliotrope, two yellow, and two heliotrope.

2. Take the yellow pair and hold the right string firmly and make two chain stitches on it, then take the left yellow string and make two stitches on that with the right. The stitches are really two simple button-hole stitches.

3. Separate the yellow strings and bring them across the two heliotrope strings right and left. Hold the left yellow string in a slanting direction to the left and work two button-hole stitches on it with each of the heliotrope strings, which will make a slanting bar of four beads to the left.

4. Now take the right yellow string and hold that in a slanting direction to the right and knot the two heliotrope strings each twice on it, which will make a slanting beaded bar to the right.

Compare the two bars thus worked to the upper part of the letter "O" and let children place the yellow strings in position to complete the circle. It will be noticed that the heliotrope strings cross each other naturally, and as this makes a pretty centre to the gimp the strings from the opposite side are used when knotting the lower half of circle. Bring the left yellow string across to the right over the heliotrope strings and knot each of the two strings on the left upon it twice. Next take the right yellow string and hold it across to the left and knot each of the two right heliotrope strings upon it. This completes the circle. Begin again by knotting the two yellow strings as described, and then bring the heliotrope strings down under them as before. The two strings form loops on either side of the yellow bar. The yellow strings being foundation strings in the next knotting are not seen, therefore the gimp is very pretty, composed of heliotrope circles joined by yellow bars and loops of heliotrope strings. The gimp is useful for trimming

XLVI. A ZIG-ZAG BAR.
(See Fig. 96*f*, page 145.)

Take two strings of same or different colours, double each in half and cast on. These will be the knotting threads.

Take a long string of a different colour and tie on singly. This string will be the foundation or leading string, and will be held to the left or right throughout whilst the other four strings are knotted on it. As the leading string is on the left of the working strings take it across them and hold in the right hand and knot the four strings twice to form a slanting beaded bar of eight beads.

Next hold the leader string to the left and knot the four strings again on it slanting to the left.

Repeat holding the leader across the working strings right and left until the strings are used up. The black board should show the direction of the leader each time and the name " zig-zag " be explained to interest the children. This bar, like the others without a fixed foundation, cannot be worked for more than 2 inches successfully without a transverse bar to hold it in position and give the worker a grip.

XLVII. DOUBLE SHELL GIMP.

Four strings are required for this exercise. The two centre or foundation strings might be of coarser make, if desired, but the No. 4 Macramé twine is best if the gimp is to be used as a trimming.

Cast on two strings 1½ yards in length. Double in half and loop over the bar of frame.

Take the first two strings and work nine or eleven button-hole stitches with the first string upon the second.

Push the stitches up together and spread out the button-hole edge to resemble a shell.

Take the third and fourth strings and button-hole eleven stitches with the fourth upon the third in the same manner.

The two shells thus formed are tied together by the foundation strings. Tie six chain knots, three with either string upon the other. Proceed as before to make two shells right and left and join with six chain knots, until the length required.

FIG. 97.

XLVIII. HAND-BAG OF SINGLE CHAIN (1).

Materials required.—1. Twelve small brass curtain-rings, the size of a halfpenny.

2. Macramé twine No. 4 in two colours, thirty-six strings, 1½ yards in length.

Method.—Cut the string into lengths by winding round the length of the desk or table and cut through all the strands at once. Distribute one ring and three lengths of string to each child. Upon each ring cast on the three strings thus: pass the two ends up through the ring and bring them over and down through the loop. Each ring will have six working strings.

Thread the rings upon a stick, and if a penny round blind-stick as long as the desk be obtained then the ends can be fixed in the upright iron work at either end of the desk, and two children can work together until the bag is complete. The knotting will be worked straight across row by row, and the last string of each alternate row will be left because this and the first will have to be knotted together to tie the bag into circular shape.

First row.—Tie eight alternate knots with right and left hand on every pair of strings.

Second row.—Take the right string of first pair and knot to the left string of second pair. Divide each pair and knot all the row in this way.

Third row.—Knot together all the pairs that were knotted in first row.

Fourth row.—Knot the same as second row.

Continue knotting these alternate rows until the depth is sufficient for a bag, then take the piece, fold together, and tie the loose strings left at the end of every row together to make in circular form. At the bottom tie the strings across and cut off the ends. The bag may be lined if desired or used as it is with simply a running string through the loops or rings. The running string may be a long piece of the same chain.

XLIX.   CHAIN BAG (2).   (Fig. 99.)

Materials required.—1. Red and cream macramé string.

2. Slate Frame, or Knotting Frame No. 2.

3. Stout macramé cord.

Method.—This is another way of making a string bag, and several children might make it at one time as the plan is so simple.

Tie round the width of the frame a single or double

red cord of coarse make like that used by the teacher for
demonstration. Upon this cord let the child work one of
the flat knots already taught, such as the Solomon's or
Genoese knots, entirely round to form a heading to the

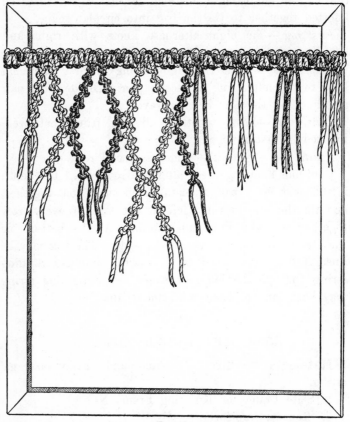

FIG. 98.

top of the bag. Let the knotting be in two colours, and
with the red cord peeping between a very effective pattern
is obtained. Two cords tied on separately and the ends

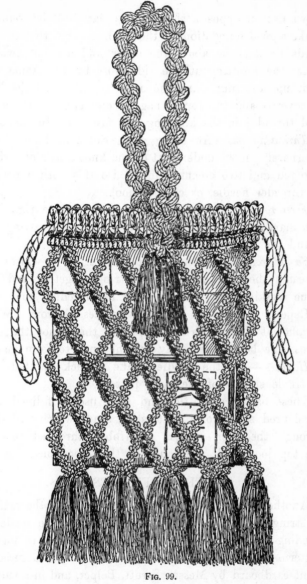

Fig. 99.

sewn flat on opposite sides of the slate will be found to make a good foundation for the heading. See that the two cords lie flat one above the other and are not twisted. Start the knotting at one side close by the frame, and continue knotting round the opposite side until the band is covered and the top of bag is complete. With needle and thread join the knotting and fasten off the ends.

Threading on.—At every sixth Solomon knot thread alternately on the under part of the knot a pair of strings, two red and two cream strings. Do this with a bodkin, or threader needle, or crochet hook.

First row.—Make six chain knots with the right and left hands respectively upon every pair of strings all round the bag.

Second row.—Tie a half knot (red string to white) just to catch the different coloured strings together and continue working the same pairs as in preceding row.

Repeat the process for every successive row. When a sufficient depth has been worked then knot the ends across the bottom and fray out the ends to form tassels.

Handles.—For the handles make a thick knotted cord of treble strings of the same pattern.

These bags are prettier and more useful if lined with a coloured sateen of a contrasting shade which will show through the open spaces. A ribbon threaded through the top loops will add much to the appearance.

STRING FRAMES.

Another useful occupation in string work is the making of string frames and baskets. The frames are made by winding regularly over a cardboard foundation to form a pattern. The shapes or foundations are manufactured in stout cardboard by Messrs. Strutt, Belper, and in a variety of shapes and sizes. Quite recently the "Scholars'" frames have been manufactured by them which are small and easy for tiny fingers to hold, so that this occupation could well be graded in difficulty for two or more classes of children engaged in the occupation.

Coloured crochet cotton is best for the small frames and fine macramé twine for the larger kind. The designs may be varied by using different coloured strings to form a pattern or by commencing to wind at different points of the frame. The two frames to be recommended for children are the "Star" and "Circular" frames.

The "Star" frame has eight points, one of which is held in the hand, whilst three are always enclosed each time in the winding. In the "Circular" frame the pattern is always started from the angles and worked outwards, which produces a raised centre and low edge to the frame. The successive winds form a very pretty round centre. The opposite effect would be produced by starting at the points, but not with so good results. These frames are useful for mounting any good hand-work. Great care needs to be taken in the choice of colours. A wise rule is to wind with strings in harmony with the centre picture.

The border is narrowed or widened according to the number of points taken in winding. If a small number be taken, then the border will be narrow and the centre large; and if nine or more points be taken, then the border will be wide and the centre small. A teacher must judge how many points to enclose to suit the size of the centre chosen. Small circular cards for children are made in thin cardboard and wound in cotton.

String weaving and its application to useful articles is very fully worked out in a former book, *Varied Occupations in Weaving*, published by Messrs. Macmillan & Co.

L. STRING PICTURE FRAME.

Materials required.—1. Strutt's fine twine, No. 10, or Strutt's crochet cotton.   2. Frame No. 1 of the star shape.   3. Brass-headed nails.   4. Picture for centre. 5. Large brown paper bag, with name affixed.

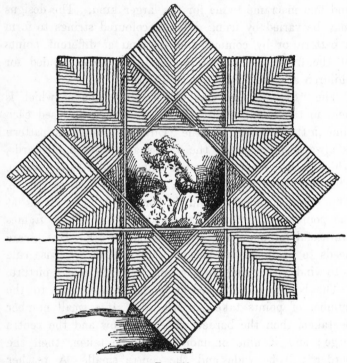

FIG. 100.

Frame.—A star of eight equal points, formed by a square placed across a square.   Lead children to see this, and dot the outline of the two separate squares on the blackboard.

Centre.—A photograph placed under a square of glass

and tied in position until the winding is finished. Pierce four holes through the foundation, and thread the string through them and tie at back.

Winding.—Push a small brass-headed nail into each point to keep the strings from slipping off, because this pattern begins *at the points* and works towards the corner. Tie the string round the three points, keeping the knot at the back, and let the first row lie quite at the edge from point to point. Wind three or four threads on this section, then turn the star one point and take the next set of three, and continue to wind in this manner all round the star. One colour may be used for the entire frame, but a variety is very effective. This is managed by knotting on a *different* colour for the *eight* different sides. The different colour used must be wound on the same side at each successive winding. The illustration was worked in two colours, viz. brown and pink, and the alternate colours were used each time the star was turned, giving alternate corners of pink and brown. After the star has been wound all round (three or four threads) at the outer edge continue in a similar way round the star again, beginning with first colour, and let all successive windings lie close to the last, and so continue until the rows of string quite fit into the corners, and the star points are completely covered.

The frequent joining of the colours may be a little troublesome, but if the children have a knowledge of star-winding and are taught to knot their own strings together, this pattern need present no difficulty if each child is provided with the necessary balls of string and brown paper bag. Finish off the last end by tying it securely to the string at back.

Cut a cardboard stand, and cover in leather paper.

Make a hinge of leather or material, and fasten to cardboard stand, and to the top of star at the back. The frame is suitable then for standing on a table, or if desired, can be suspended by cord or ribbon. The pattern described gives a raised centre, graduating lower *towards* the points, but the reverse effect is obtained by starting at the corners, and winding *outwards* to the points.

Although the winding is similar and easy for the children, two different colours will give quite a changed appearance to the pattern.

LI. PATTERNS.

Pattern 1.—Star of eight equal points. Begin in the angle or corner, and wind six threads outwards towards the points in one colour, turn and repeat on all seven sides. A second colour may be used or not in the succeeding rounds.

Pattern 2.—Begin at angles and wind towards points, using six threads and alternate colours *each round*.

Pattern 3.—Begin at corners and wind towards the points, and use a different colour for the second section or side. Alternate the two colours each time the card is turned, thus producing four sides and four corners of one colour and four sides and four corners of another.

Pattern 4.—Begin at corners, wind towards the points, and use eight different colours, one for each side, keeping *one colour* to the *same* side throughout.

LII. CARD BASKET.

Materials required.—1. Large star, cut in pliable cardboard, measuring 10 inches from point to point. 2. Blue balls of crochet cotton. 3. Yellow-tinted picture. 4. Crystal headed pins. 5. Ball of silver tinsel.

The foundation must be cut in pliable cardboard, so

that the points may be gradually pulled up as the weaving nears the points.

This pretty basket is wound in pale blue crochet cotton, according to pattern No. 1. Fix a Christmas card in the centre with gum, and then tie the cotton round

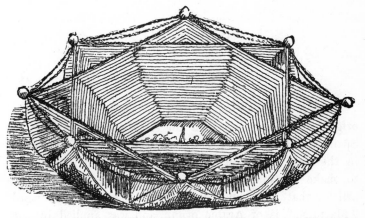

Fig. 101.

the section, with knot at back, and let the first thread lie exactly *in the corner*. Weave six threads each time, and continue winding the whole star in the one colour. As the weaving proceeds the points must be pulled up-wards, and a crystal-headed pin stuck in each point to keep the winding intact. The last row of winding is of silver tinsel, and this is *twisted round* the pin each time and carried twice round from point to point to form a loop edge.

Any of the *reverse* patterns 1, 2, 3, 4, are suitable for this basket, but are not so pretty if wound in more than one or two colours. The basket is suitable to stand on a dressing-table, or it could be hung up as a novel picture frame. A fancy handle of cardboard wound in cotton and tinsel can be added if desired.

STAGE III.

MACRAMÉ.

What it is.—Macramé or knotted lace is of very ancient origin, and was much used for ecclesiastical purposes in Spain and Italy in the sixteenth century. It was made in the time of Queen Mary on a pillow, and was used to make ornamental covers for hand-bags and other articles that were lined with coloured silks. The word "Macramé" is of Arabic origin and was applied by the Italians to the ornamental fringe produced by knotting the ends of their coarse towels; but, as bands, square strips, and headings can be worked as well as fringes, a more appropriate term for the work is "Knotting." The macramé twines now manufactured for the purpose may be obtained in several degrees of coarseness, and in the most delicate and beautiful artistic shades, according to the work required.

The board.—For school use a long narrow deal board with a lath nailed at each end on its upper surface will answer the purpose. There will be no need of nails upon which to tie the strings because a better plan is to knot the foundation cords entirely round the board. By this arrangement a child can be engaged upon a piece of work twice the length of the board, because the cords can be twisted round to the under side when the upper side of the board is full, or the board could be turned over and worked on the under side without shifting the strings if a small strip of wood be inserted just to raise the strings. The foundation cords must be strained on very tightly, they should be knotted through a loop and made secure by a slip knot at the left-hand side of the board, because the work proceeds from left to right as it is worked.

Those intending to take up the occupation should procure No. 3 Anyon bracket board made in plain deal wood, and fitted with cross bars and screw ends at 2s. 6d. each, but doubtless at a reduction if buying a quantity. It is a great improvement upon the plain board, because it is provided at each end with cross bars of coarse wire upon which the foundation cords are tied, and this saves a large amount of trouble to the teacher because she is able to string the boards full from the first and tighten the work from time to time as it gets loose, by a simple contrivance fixed at the end for screwing up the foundation cords. These boards are only half a yard in length, and thus enable two children to work side by side in the same desk. They never get out of order, and are a great saving of time to the teacher, who needs to get them fully strung at the start and her preparation is at an end. The children can help in this preparation, each child can tie its strings on the bars and the teacher need only screw them to the requisite tightness. The boards can be scrubbed with soap and water once a year and be started fresh and new looking for each new set of children taking the subject.

In working some of the open knots and large patterns it is necessary to fix the part to the board, and strong

pins are sold for the purpose. Instead of using pins the
teacher can lightly fasten the part with a small tin tack,
this plan has been found to answer better than pins,
because the tack holds the work with more security and
does not come out when pulled, as is the case with the
pins. The tacks must be carefully put in *between* the
stitches and not *through* the string.

USES OF KNOTTING.

The work can be applied to making many useful
articles, *e.g.* :

1. Fringes for counterpanes, towels, toilet-covers,
dresses, etc.
2. Fringes for brackets, and occasional tables.
3. Fringes for mantel borders.
4. Fringes for altar cloths and dress-trimmings in silk.
5. Fringes for wall-pockets and toilet tidies.
6. Squares for tea-cosies and cushions.
7. Squares for handkerchief cases and night-dress cases.
8. Strips for work and hand-bags.
9. Strips for antimacassars or furniture decorations.
10. Cords for knotted long or short window-curtains.
11. Cords for toy whips and reins.
12. Cords for watch chains and the centres of mats, etc.

As a rule boys produce better work than girls, because
they have a firmer grip and are more used to tightening
knots in string, but the girls are more interested in
working out new patterns, and their work is much fresher
and more correct than that of the boys.

After working through the exercises given for the first
half of the year the children will be able to reproduce
any of them and design patterns for fringes, etc. In

fact if a definite name be given to each exercise the teacher will find that the quick children can reproduce an exercise from the name only, thus : "Make a double star of six strings," or "Make a bar of eight Solomon's knots." The children are very fond of the Solomon knot and no doubt the name is the great attraction. After every lesson the boards should be overlooked to see that the work is ready for continuation, as it may happen that the foundation cords need tightening, or a child might have missed a lesson, if so, during the interval from one lesson to the next—which in the writer's school is one week—occasion should be taken when overlooking the boards to let any backward child get up to the rest of the class. This may easily be done by letting a proficient child teach the little delinquent, or by letting a pupil teacher give the instruction needed. A good rule is to allow boards only to regular children and give the others a slate frame as a punishment, this plan was found to answer admirably and to keep all the class at the same standard of efficiency. It has been erroneously remarked that macramé lace cannot be taught to large classes ; this statement was evidently made by a theorist who has never had the experience of teaching large classes, as, since the occupation is essentially one of demonstration teaching, with everything in readiness the teacher can demonstrate to a class of thirty or sixty as well as she could to a class of ten. In the writers' school thirty-six little girls between six and seven years have been taken in Stage III. knotting for the first time for the past eight years, without having previously passed through Stages I. and II., and at the end of a year have been able to work any exercise in Stages II. or III., and copy any pattern of the same if illustrated on the blackboard. If a series of large wall sheets of these patterns were published for class use they would be of immense advantage to the teacher, for when the knot is once known the child becomes independent of the teacher and when started on a pattern can proceed without further help. It is advisable to keep all the class at the same stage of the exercises upon the teaching boards and when the task appointed for the lesson has been accomplished by the sharper children to allow these to help the weaker ones, because a little child will often make a difficulty clearer to another child than the teacher. As the exercises advance this help will not be so much needed; then supplementary work must be provided for the quick workers. If each pupil have a second board upon which to reproduce any pattern already taught, the child will be no trouble to the teacher because it knows the pattern and can keep working it on the full length of its own board. In this way many good specimens of the work are reproduced as fringes for brackets by the clever children long before one half of the year has passed. The plodders are still being helped forward by the teacher without any detriment to the sharp ones.

A piece of unbleached calico should be tacked along the entire length of the board and folded over the work and tucked under to keep it clean and free from dust. Each child's name should be written on a slip of paper and pasted on the top of the board. Constant inspection whilst the children are at work, and the mention of any little faults in the work such as "too loose," "too slanting," etc., will prevent bad work, and unpicking. As an instance of how much the work is liked by the children, many have borrowed a board for "father to see" and several have bought string and produced most creditable work at home for Sunday School competitions.

TERMS USED IN MACRAMÉ

The terms used in the construction of Macramé lace are :

1. *Foundation Cords.*—These are the cords that run across the board lengthways from left to right and upon which the working strings are built up and held in position. They should be of a coarser make than the working strings or else the ordinary string should be used double. They may be several in number, according to the depth of the pattern being worked. To make their purpose understood by children the teacher should compare them to the foundation of a house and lead them to see that upon them the stability of the work depends and each successive cord might be compared to the various floors of a house.

The foundation cords separate one series of knots from another, and they should be cut the length of the lace required, and strained very tightly across the board, or no good work can be done.

2. *The Leader.*—In working, one string is always held tight in the direction the knots have to go, whilst the other strings are worked upon it. The tightened string is called the "Leader," as it has to be held in whatever direction the knots are to be worked. The knotting thread and the leader are constantly changing places as the work progresses, knots having to be made now with one and now with the other ; *e.g.*, when a leaf or pattern is worked from right to left the leader is held in the left hand across the other working strings and *vice versa*. This holding of the leader *across* the other working strings

is always the stumbling-block to the children, because it is not always the same string and they often forget to take it across *the top of the others*. To simplify matters and impress which string is to be called the "leader," compare the string to a child leading in marching and point out that the course he takes all the others follow, and at the same time tell the children that the next child to the leader is like the next string to the "leader," and is always called the *first*—always the first string to be knotted. Let the children repeat at every oppor- tunity, "The first string is always the one next to the leader" until the fact is thoroughly known, as this is the only point in Stage III. that the children do not at first understand.

3. *Working Threads.*—The Knotting or Working Thread is the one with which the knot is made, and each string is knotted twice. Each string being doubled in half when casting on makes two working threads. When working a pattern the strings should be cut twice the depth in length and as many cast on as will be required to work one scallop of the pattern. In the elementary exercises on the board it is best to give six strings of a different colour for each distinct exercise; this will give twelve working strings, and no exercise at first will need more working strings than twelve.

4. *Bars.*—A Bar is referred to in macramé as a vertical arrangement of knots. Bars are generally used for the lighter portions of a pattern. They may be made with two, three, or four strings, according to the thickness required, and are described in Stage II.

5. *Diamonds and Stars.*—A Diamond or Star is made by holding the leaders in a slanting direction and covering with macramé knots. Four leaders are covered in this

way to form the four sides of the diamond or points of the star. Both are made with single, double, and treble sides.

RULES FOR MACRAMÉ KNOTTING.

Rule 1. To work each knot evenly and of the same tightness throughout.

Rule 2. To draw each knot close up to the last.

Rule 3. To keep each thread as it is worked exactly under the place where it was cast on.

Rule 4. To keep all the working threads lying down in the order in which they have to be worked.

Rule 5. To hold the "foundation string" or "leader" perfectly straight and tight, while the working strings are being knotted upon it.

Rule 6. To hold the "foundation string" or "leader" *upon* and *across* the working strings.

Rule 7. To give a definite position for the "leader" hand to rest so that the same distance apart will be preserved when repeating the pattern.

CASTING ON.

I. CASTING ON WITH ONE STRING.

Preparation.—The children's boards must all be prepared with four foundation cords tightly strained across. These strings are to be named respectively first, second, third, and fourth foundation cords. The name should be written upon the blackboard and, to make their purpose understood by the children, the teacher should compare them to the foundation of a house, and lead them to see that upon them the stability of the work depends, and that is why a coarser make of string is used for them. Each successive cord might be likened to the different floors of a house and thus interest the children in their new work.

Distribute six red strings, 1 yard in length, to each child. The working strings must not be too short or the child can get no grip in tightening the work. Give the term " working strings," and write the word on blackboard, and explain to children that they are so called because all the knots are made with them and, therefore, they do all the work.

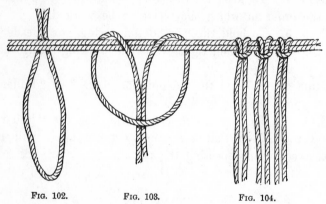

Fig. 102.   Fig. 103.   Fig. 104.

Question upon the colour of the string. (Red.) Let children name any things of a red colour. How many strings are there? Six. Double each one in half, how many are there now? Twelve. What length is each string now? Half a yard. How many half yards in 1 yard? How many in 6 yards? etc.

Lesson.—The teacher must have a rope strained across the blackboard, and with a coarse make of red macramé cord she should work every step with the children.

1. Take one working string doubled in half. Show.

2. Pass the two ends *upwards, under* the top foundation cord (Fig. 102).

3. Draw the ends *over* the cord and *down* through the loop (Fig. 103).

Repeat the process for each thread and draw each one down tightly (Fig. 104). This exercise is quickly learnt and is called simple "casting on," but when the children have advanced in the work they will be able to cast on with picot headings. After correctly casting on the six strings of red, six more of another colour should be given for them to repeat the exercise.

II. CASTING ON WITH TWO STRINGS.

For large pieces of work the following is a quicker way of casting on:

The exercise is worked exactly like the preceding one, two strings being used instead of one.

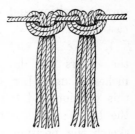

Fig. 105.

1. Take two strings of equal length (1 yard), double in half to find the centre.

2. Pass the four ends up under the first foundation cord and bring them over down through the double loop and pull tight. See that the strings lie flat and in their correct position.

Each casting on gives four working strings (Fig. 105).

III. THE MACRAMÉ KNOT.

The macramé knot is very simple, and consists really of two plain button-hole stitches worked over a cord which is called the "leader." In the working of macramé the "leader" will have to be held by the child whilst making the knots, and so that two difficulties should not be presented at the same time, it is advisable, when teaching the subject to young children, to teach the knot first upon a tightened foundation cord, so that the child has only the difficulty of the knot to overcome. When the children have learnt "to cast on," and have twelve working strings already on their boards, then begin to teach the macramé knot. There will be no difficulty whatever if the children have passed through Stages I. and II.

Lesson.—See that the second foundation cord on the board is pushed up close to the first. It must lie *upon* the top of the working threads, therefore the children must pull down their strings under it and see all are in correct position and each string lying down in order of casting on.

1. Take the end of first string and carry it across the others and lay the end upon the cord about 3 inches along. Let all the class place their strings in this position and tell them this step is called "forming the loop"; point out what is meant by "the loop," and sketch the position on blackboard so that children can compare and see their strings are right.

2. Pass the end OVER and UNDER the foundation cord and let it come INSIDE the loop. The children are prone to bring the end *outside* the loop instead of *inside*, and make no knot whatever, but if the position of the string is given in a series of steps for each new knot, the children quickly understand and follow, and their progress and good work will be most marked, and amply repay the care taken at first.

3. Pull the end down through the loop. Repeat 1, 2, 3, with the SAME string, and the knot is complete (Fig. 106). The great point in making the knot is to get the stitches equal, to do this the first half of the knot must be pulled tightly in position before the second half is worked. Compare the knot to two threaded beads of equal size. Every working thread is knotted twice and forms two beads, if this fact be impressed upon the children and simple calculations given, such as : How many beads will four strings make ? How many six ? etc. ; and the

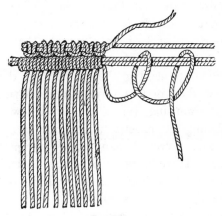

FIG. 106.

children be called upon to count the number of beads worked by the teacher upon her board and then to count their own, they will soon find out whether they have worked correctly. Probably they have missed some string in its turn, or perhaps knotted some strings only once instead of twice, which is a common fault at first until the children are in the habit of counting their beads. The teacher should question upon the number of beads that will be made in each successive exercise, and then a child is able to judge of the accuracy of its own work. Children should repeat at the commencement of every lesson "Each string must be knotted twice." The work must be examined by the teacher and corrected by the child before another exercise is attempted. The quick, clever children might have another set of strings of different colour "to cast on" and "knot" whilst the teacher gives her attention to the backward ones. The different colours please the children and simplify the instructions, because the commands can be made much more definite, and they form a ready means of adding, subtracting, and dividing. As this exercise is the basis of the macramé work, it is advisable that the children should be kept at it till regularity and tightness have been obtained in making the knots. All the foundation cords are worked in this way, and the strings arranged in order for working a new pattern below. Every two stitches should lie exactly under its own threads on the *first* cord, however many successive patterns below are worked. This second cord gives a firmness to the edge, and should be done for every large piece of work. It must be tightened close up to the first, and no string must be seen between the first and second cords.

CASTING ON WITH "PICOTS."

Macramé laces are much improved if begun with a heading of knots. These are made before the strings are "cast on," and may be varied by using any of the knots taught in previous Stages I. and II. The most simple and suitable are single and double knotted picots, and button-hole loops, and fringed headings.

IV. CASTING ON WITH A SINGLE PICOT KNOT.

1. Give out twelve strings, and double each one in half to find the middle.

2. At the middle pass the string round finger and tie a double knot. (Ex. XII., Stage I.)

3. Pull the knots up and show children, and give the name "picot." Let them prepare all their strings with picots ready for "casting on."

4. *Casting on.*—Take a string, pass the picot up under the first foundation cord, and with finger and thumb of the left hand hold it tightly to the cord in position whilst the strings are knotted on it.

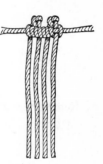

FIG. 107.

5. All picot headings are cast on in the same way, *i.e.* the strings are knotted on to the foundation cord with macramé knots, as in Ex. III. As each string is knotted it pulls the picot down close to the cord, and holds it there in position (Fig. 107). This point must be attended to with the children, because they are apt to keep the picot too far above the cord when knotting, and get a loose heading instead of a firm set of hard knots.

V. CASTING ON WITH A DOUBLE KNOTTED PICOT.

Double picots are worked with two strings instead of one, similar to the single picot.

Take two strings of equal length. Find the half, and there tie two knots with the double strings (Ex. XV., Stage I.). This makes the double picot. Pinch it into good shape before casting on.

Pass the picot under the top cord. Hold it close down to the cord, and knot all four strings in turn on to the foundation cord.

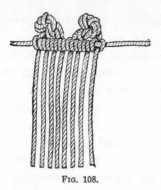

Fig. 108.

Remember each string must be knotted twice, and the picot drawn close down to the cord (Fig. 108).

VI. CASTING ON WITH BUTTON-HOLE LOOPS.

This is a very simple and pretty heading, and has already been taught in Stage I. as button-hole on fingers.

1. Take two strings, one 2 inches longer than the other. Find the centre of both.

Fig. 109.

2. Place the middle of the shorter string across the fingers of left hand, as in crochet work, and button-hole the other upon it. Or if more convenient, fasten one string to desk and loop the other upon it, taking care to keep the ends of both equal in length ready for casting on.

Work twelve or thirteen stitches according to the size of picot required.

Draw up both ends of the shorter or foundation string, and curve the button-hole stitches into a loop (Fig. 110).

It will be noticed that the drawing up strings will be in the centre of the four, and those of the button-hole edge outside, or the first and fourth strings. In this order they must be arranged and cast on.

Hold the loop under the cord, and knot on each string twice in the order mentioned above.

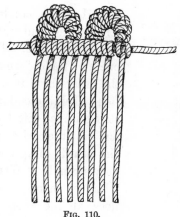

Fig. 110.

Other pretty headings may be made of the tatted bar and tatted loop bar, both of which may be drawn up and cast on in the same manner. The Solomon knot and Genoese double knots also make bold headings. The knots must be worked at the middle of the strings, and cast on like the button-hole loop picot. A simple heading is by holding one end of a string about an inch above the top cord, and casting the lower end on the foundation cord

with two macramé knots. The short end at top is frayed
out when lace is finished.   This method is useful for
insertions or bands where both edges are to be alike; it
is easy for the children to manage top and bottom.

VII.   TO WORK A BEADED BAR, OF FOUR STRINGS, TO THE LEFT.

Knotting with the right hand and holding the "leader"
with the left, seems to come most natural and easy to
the worker, so every exercise will be first taught in
this position, and then reversed, until both hands work
equally well.

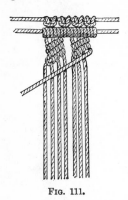

1. Let the children count four
strings and put all others quite
away from them.   Take the fourth
one as "leader" and hold it across
the other three in a slanting direction.   Tell the children to hold this
string in the left hand *very tightly*,
and rest the wrist on the corner of
the board.   Impress it upon them
very strongly at this stage that the
"leader" hand *never moves*, if it

Fig. 111.

does, all the knots will be wrong.
The children are apt to hold the leader rather slack
and produce slack work and twisted knots in conse-
quence.

2. Take the string *next* to the leader and make a
macramé knot with it upon the leader.   Pull the knot
upwards, with the right hand, so that it fits close into
the angle made by the leader.   It is best to teach the
children that the *first* string to take is *the one next to the
leader*, and when the leader is once held in position at

each exercise, the children are able to remember which string to take.

3. The left hand must still be kept in position until the other two strings are knotted and pulled tightly up to the last. When finished, the row should look like six beads.

4. When one row has been worked, hastily examine and mention any faults, and let children place the four strings down in a straight position on the board. Point out that the last leader is now the first string on the board, but that the four strings are going to take it in turns to be leader in this exercise, like four good children, whom teacher lets take turn as leader in marching.

Second row.—Take the fourth or right-hand string as before and hold across the others as leader, and knot the others upon it as taught in previous row. The working of this row will be found a little difficult to beginners, because its perfection lies in its regularity and closeness to the last row. Practice will soon overcome this little failure if the children are told where and how to hold the string which is the leader.

The leader of each succeeding row must be held across close to the last row, just as it ought to lie when knotted; if this point is attended to, and the hand held perfectly still with a tightened string, the rows will fall in their proper position.

Third row.—Place the strings in straight lying-down order on the board and work a third row like the second, taking the right-hand string as leader.

Fourth row.—Same as third. This completes the exercise.

Push up the third foundation cord to touch the lowest corner of bar, and pass all the four strings underneath it and knot on each string twice, like the foundation cord above. Take the other two sets of four red strings and make two more bars in the same way. This will be sufficient for one lesson.

VIII. TO WORK A BEADED BAR, OF FOUR STRINGS, TO THE RIGHT. (FIG. 112.)

This exercise is the exact reverse of the last, its educational benefit trains the left hand to manipulate the knots whilst the right is kept still. The left-hand, or first of the four strings, is taken as leader each time. Let the children complete three sets of bars in green string, and finish on the third foundation cord as the end of this lesson.

IX. TO WORK A BEADED BAR, OF SIX STRINGS, TO THE LEFT. (FIG. 113.)

The instructions given for Ex. VII. are precisely the same for this exercise, only that six strings are taken instead of four and, therefore, the leader will have five strings knotted on, each time making ten beads in each row. The pattern will be worked twice in the lesson.

X. TO WORK A BEADED BAR, OF SIX STRINGS, TO THE RIGHT. (FIG. 114.)

Reverse Exercise IX., working with left hand.

XI. A SINGLE DIAMOND. (FIG. 115.)

Cast on eight strings, this will give sixteen working strings. Eight strings will be required for the pattern. Arrange the threads upon the second cord as in preceding

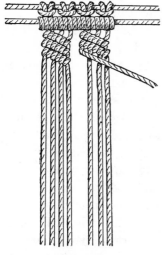

FIG. 112.

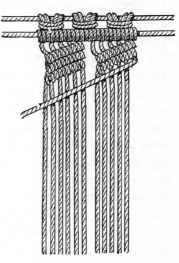

FIG. 113.

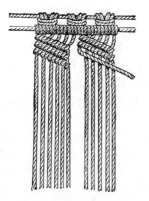

FIG. 114.

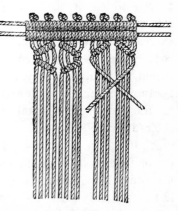

FIG. 115.

exercises, and, if a large pattern is to be worked, two cords should be knotted, as in illustration.

Left half of diamond.—Take the first four strings, hold the fourth as leader in the left hand across 1, 2, 3, and in a slanting direction, and work a beaded bar as taught in Ex. VII. Keep the same leader but transfer it to the right hand *above* the strings and knot the same strings on it again in a slanting direction to the right. The teacher must demonstrate the course of this leader upon the blackboard. If the children are not watched they will go wrong where the leader turns back, and try to knot without first bringing their strings straight down before changing the course of the leader. These faults are pointed out for the benefit of the inexperienced teacher who will often be puzzled to find out how the work is wrong, and if extra attention is given to these common faults much time will be saved in unpicking. This completes one side of the diamond. Take the next four strings for the corresponding half of the diamond. Sketch the complete diamond upon the blackboard, and call upon the children to tell which of the next four strings will have to be taken as leader to complete the pattern. These mental exercises are most beneficial, and train the children to copy patterns drawn upon the blackboard. In fact the inventive faculty is very largely developed in this stage, because children are allowed to invent patterns, or make up the same of horizontal, vertical, or oblique lines upon their drawing slates.

Right half of diamond.—Take the first string of the next set of four, hold it in the right hand as leader, and knot the other three strings upon it. Change the leader into the left hand, place all the strings in order under it, and knot a beaded bar slanting to the left to meet the leader of the first half. Slip the strings under the foundation cord and knot all eight strings, as in previous exercises. See that the stitches are exactly under those of the foundation cord above.

XII. A DOUBLE DIAMOND WITH FILLED CENTRE.

Cast on eight strings, and knot over second foundation cord. This diamond is worked precisely the same as the single diamond, except that each side is composed of double bars, and the top half is worked first instead of left side.

Take the first four strings, hold the *fourth* in left hand across the first three, and work macramé knots upon it with them (Ex. VII.).

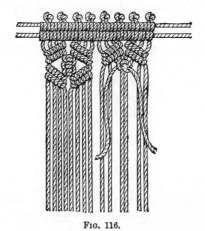

Fig. 116.

Leave that leader and take the right-hand or fourth again of that set as leader and work a second beaded bar just below it (Ex. VII.).

Take the *first* string of the next four as leader and

slant it towards the right, and work macramé knots to form two-beaded bars. This completes the top half of the diamond (Ex. VIII.).

Centre knot.—If desired a fancy knot can be made in the centre before the lower half of the diamond is worked. Knots suitable for this are the double button-hole and "Solomon" knots. To make the knot in the centre, take the four centre threads, two from each side, and work a Solomon knot. Hold the two centre threads straight down, whilst the knot is made with the first and fourth strings. If the children find any difficulty in making the knot, without having the two centre strings held in position, then let them pin these straight to their dress, or temporarily tie to next foundation cord whilst the knot is worked, because children need both hands to make this knot. This done, take the leader that was last used on the left side and hold it in a slanting direction towards the right, over the other strings, and make a slanting double-beaded bar of three strings. Then take the leader last used on the right, hold it across to the left, and work a double-beaded bar. The diamond is complete, and the strings are then worked upon the third foundation cord to finish the lesson.

XIII. A TRIPLE DIAMOND WITH FILLED CENTRE.

The large patterns of triple stars or diamonds are always worked immediately beneath a foundation cord, because the strings proceed in regular order, and the cord gives a firmness to this heavy pattern.

Twelve or sixteen strands are generally taken for triple stars or diamonds.

The triple diamond is worked exactly like the double

diamond of preceding exercise, only three bars are made on every side instead of two. The top half is worked first. Three slanting bars to the left with six strings (Ex. IX.); three slanting bars to the right with six strings (Ex. X.), which completes the top half.

1. For the centre take the four middle strings, two from each half.

2. Hold the centre two and make half a Solomon's knot with the first and fourth.

3. Tie a knot on the two centre strings (Fig. 117).

4. Work Solomon's knot below this central knot.

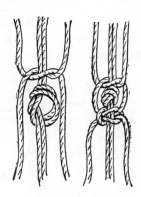

Fig. 117.

The lower half of diamond is now worked like the top half.

Take the last leader on the left and slant to the right and work three bars (Ex. X.).

Then take the last leader on the right and hold to the left, and again work three bars (Ex. IX.).

The diamond is complete, and the strings must be cast on to the next foundation cord unless a series of diamonds are to be worked, as in fringe, Fig. 127. When casting on to the foundation cord the *point* of the diamond only touches the cord, and the strings increase in length from the point.

Note.—It might be as well to mention, so as to prevent errors in future patterns, that the strands or working threads in macramé lace are constantly changing places, and therefore cannot retain their original or starting number. At the beginning of every row, or bar, or design, the working threads are re-numbered each time, beginning at 1 and so on, and will have no reference whatever to any preceding number they might have borne.

XIV. A SINGLE STAR.

The star is but a variation of the diamond, that is, it is a diamond reversed and begun with the *first* or left-hand string instead of the *fourth*.

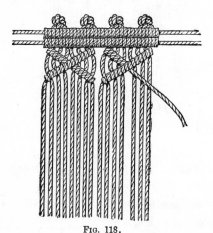

Fig. 118.

1. Take the *first* string in the right hand as leader, and slant to the right lower corner of the board. Hold it firmly in position, and knot with macramé knots the second, third, and fourth strings upon it.

2. Then take the eighth string, or the fourth of next set, as leader, slant it towards the left corner of board, and work macramé knots with the seventh, sixth, and fifth strings in succession.

3. Keep the same string as leader, and work also upon it after the others, the strings of first set in order. This gives a long centre cross-bar of *fourteen* beads (Fig. 118).

4. This done, only one point of star is now wanting. Take the fifth string and hold it to the right as leader *over* the last three, and knot six beads, or three macramé knots, upon it to complete the star.

XV. A DOUBLE STAR.

This exercise is made like the single star.

1. Count the first four strings and take *first* one as leader. Slant the leader to the right over the second, third, and fourth strings, and knot these upon it in consecutive order with macramé knots.

Place the strings down in order, and again take the first or left-hand string as leader and hold across to the right and knot again a second bar, as in Ex. VIII. This second leader was the second string when starting, but as before mentioned, every new row is re-numbered as the strings come in order. One corner of star is now finished.

2. Take the next four strings and hold the *fourth* across the other three, slanting to the left, and work six beads, or macramé knots, upon it. (A macramé knot makes two beads.)

Arrange the strings in order as they come from the bar, and take the fourth or right-hand string again and hold across *all* the strings. There will be *seven* strings to knot this time, and care must be taken that when knotting on the middle string or first of next set the star must be pulled tightly at the centre so that the top corner fits closely to the cross-bar.

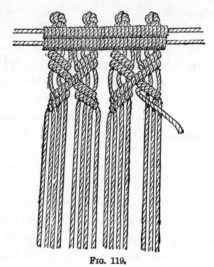

FIG. 119.

3. When this long bar is worked count back four strings, and hold the fourth to the left parallel with long bar, and work the short side of bottom left corner.

4. Take the other four strings on the right and work a double bar to the right (Ex. VIII.).

XVI. TREBLE STAR WITH RAISED CENTRE.

Large stars, formed of three and four bars for each point, are generally finished with a handsome raised picot in the centre.

The picot is formed of a series of Solomon or Genoese knots worked with the four centre strings, and then looped to form a raised picot.

The upper half of star is worked first.

Pattern.—*The Star.*—Take sixteen strings for each star, and work a beaded bar three times, slanting to the right with the first eight strings, as in Ex. x., and then three beaded bars slanting to the left with the next eight strings. This completes the upper half of the diamond.

The Picot.—Take the two leader strands which were last used for the right and left bars, and fasten them down to the board or front of child's dress. Then take the next string on either side of the two held down, and work ten or twelve Solomon knots. About 1½ inches of knotting is required for the picot.

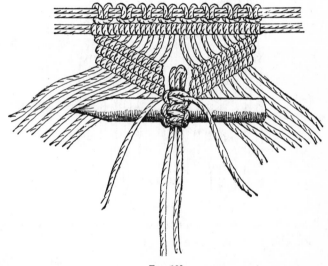

Fɪɢ. 120.

Looping of the Picot.—Place a pencil horizontally across the bar just worked, and take the two centre strands and pass upwards over the pencil and down through the opening of the diamond. Bring the strings out below the pencil, and tie each string to its own working string,

right and left. Remove the pencil, and work the lower
half of the star.

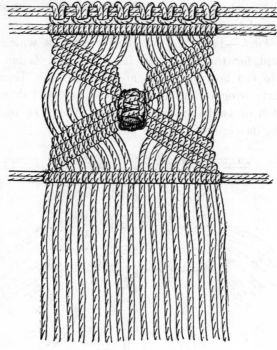

FIG. 121.

Take the same two centre strands as leaders right and
left for the first bar on each side.

PATTERNS COMBINING STAGES I. AND II

SUPPLEMENTARY EXERCISES.

Many of the quick workers who learn their new exercises
in Stage III. before the majority of the class, should be

given supplementary work, consisting of exercises taught
in the previous Stages. These are all suitable for the
insertion portion of heavy or deep fringes, because the
beaded bar patterns of Stage III. are mostly introduced
in the centre and lower part of macramé lace. Therefore,
if the strings are cut sufficiently long to allow of a lower
pattern being added, the three open ones here given
could be worked to form the top of a fringe, and any of
the beaded bar patterns added below.

The great value of the horizontal foundation cords is
that they rearrange all the strings in regular working
order, and any new pattern can be started after a cord.

Large stars and diamonds with a bar on either side form
handsome patterns to introduce after either of the following insertions, and would be suitable for mantel border or
bracket fringes.

PATTERNS MADE OF EXERCISES IN STAGES I. AND II.

XVII. INSERTION OF GENOESE AND BANNISTER BAR PATTERNS.

Preparation.—The frame must be strung with four
foundation cords. The strings cut 1 yard in length.

Casting on.—Take two strings and tie together about
1 inch from the ends.

Foundation cord.—Hold the knot under the top foundation cord and cast on each string twice, with a macramé
knot (Ex. IV., Stage III.). Repeat for each string.

Second row.—A bar of three Genoese knots, right and
left alternately. Take every set of four strings; hold the
second and third strings, and knot with the first and
fourth alternately (Ex. IX., Stage II.).

Third row.—Foundation cord of macramé knots (Ex. III., Stage III.).

Fourth or *centre row.*—Cross bars of bannister knots. Take four strings and work twisted bars of twenty knots (Ex. XIX., Stage II.). Repeat the exercise with every four strings.

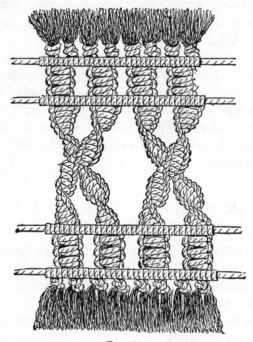

Fig. 122.

Fifth row.—When casting on the strings from bannister bar, cross the bars right over left, and take those proceeding from the second bar first and cast on.

Sixth row.—Same as second.

Seventh row.—Same as first. The ends are frayed out top and bottom.

XVIII.—FRINGE WITH BUTTON-HOLE HEADING.

Preparation.—The boards or frames must be strung with five foundation cords, and the strings cut 1½ yards in length.

Heading.—Take two strings, find the half, and button-hole eight stitches across the fingers (Ex. VI.). Draw up to form loop. Cast on first cord.

Foundation cord.

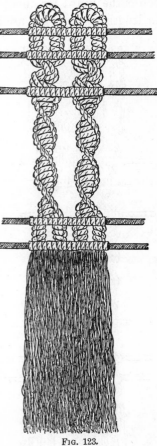

First pattern.—A bar of three single button-hole stitches to the left with first and second strings, and a bar of three button-hole stitches to the right with third and fourth strings. Repeat for every four strings (Ex. I. and II., Stage II.).

Foundation cord.—(Ex. III., Fig. 106).

Second pattern.—Bar of four double chain knots. Repeat with every four strings (Ex. XLIII., Stage II.).

Foundation cord.—(Ex. III., Fig. 106).

Third pattern.—Long bars of bannister knot (Ex. XIX., Stage II.). Twenty knots in each bar.

Fig. 123.

Foundation cord.—(Ex. III., Fig. 106).

Fourth pattern.—Single button-hole bars, same as first pattern.

Foundation cord.—(Ex. III., Fig. 106). *Fringe.*

XIX.—INSERTION WITH KNOTTED ENDS FOR CURTAIN BANDS.

Preparation.—Six foundation cords must be strung across the board for this pattern. Cut the strings 1 yard in length, as they are used singly.

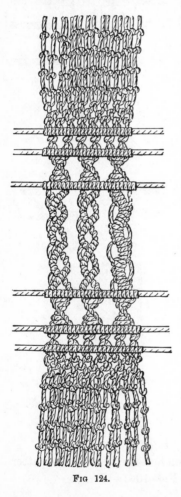

Fig 124.

Casting on.—Take a string, pass about 8 inches under the top cord. Hold the string and cord together with finger and thumb of left hand, like holding a picot, and then make a macramé knot with the long end. When the board is full, all these ends of 8 inches are knotted together with single chain knots for three rows, and the separate ends knotted with single knots, like a short fringe.

Second pattern.—Small bars of two single chain knots (Ex. XLI., Stage II.).

Foundation cord.—(Ex. III., Fig. 106.).

Third pattern.—Bars of eight bannister knots (Ex. XIX., Stage II.).

Foundation cord.—(Ex. III., Fig. 106).

Centre pattern.—A waved bar of six shells (Ex. XVII., Stage II.). Two beaded bars of *four* strings made of small single stars (Ex. XIV.).

Foundation cord.—(Ex. III.).

Fifth pattern.—Same as third.

Foundation cord.—(Ex. III.).

Sixth pattern.—Same as second.

Foundation cord.—(Ex. III.).

Fringe.—Knotted with three rows of alternate chain knots, and the ends separately knotted.

PATTERNS COMBINING EXERCISES IN STAGE III.

As soon as the children can make a diamond or star accurately, it is as well to give them an easy pattern combining the exercises to work the whole length of their board, during which time the teacher can give individual attention to the backward ones. Any of the following patterns are easy to a child who has worked through the exercises, and only a slight variation in the working is needed to quite alter the effect of the pattern. Many of the patterns here given have been put together by the children themselves after having gone through the exercises. In fact Stage III. should, as far as possible, cultivate and develop the power to design.

XX. A FRINGE OF TWO PATTERNS OF BEADED STARS.

Preparation.—*Boards* strung with four foundation cords. *Strings* cut 1½ yards in length, which when doubled will give ¾ yard for knotting.

Pattern.—*First row.*—Cast on with single strings (Ex. I.).

Second row.—Foundation cord of macramé knots (Ex. III.).

Third row.—An insertion made of single stars (Ex. XIV.).

1. Take four strings for every small star.

2. Hold the first string slanting to the right as leader, and knot the second twice upon it.

3. Take the fourth string and hold slanting to the left as leader, and knot the third, and second, and first strings on it. This gives the continuous centre bar.

4. Take the two right-hand strings and knot the fourth upon the third to give the lower point of star.

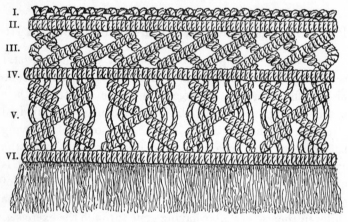

FIG. 125.

Take every four strings, number them as 1, 2, 3, 4, and continue these small stars straight across the board.

Another row of stars is made exactly in the same way below the others, and the leader from the long cross-bar of previous stars is held across the centre of the lower set of stars, and thus one continuous bar passes through both sets of stars.

Children could be taught to do these long bars entirely at once, and work the four corners from each after, but it is found easier to call the pattern "two single stars," which the children know how to work, instead of teaching another way.

Fourth row.—Foundation cord of macramé knots.

Fifth row.—Double pointed star of eight strings (Ex. xv.).

Sixth row.—Foundation cord of macramé knots. Strings cut and frayed as short fringe.

XXI. FRINGE OF THREE PATTERNS OF BEADED BARS AND DIAMONDS.

This pattern is slightly different to the preceding one. The large pattern is a double diamond with filled centre instead of the double pointed star in previous pattern.

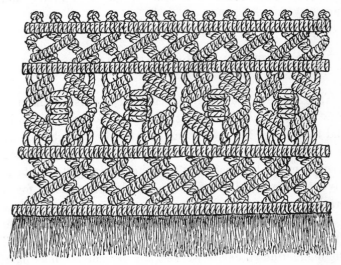

Fig. 126.

Preparation.—*Board* strung with *four* foundation cords. *Strings* cut 1½ yards in length and knotted with single picot.

First row.—Casting on with picots (Ex. IV., Fig. 107).

Second row.—Insertion of small single stars (Ex. XIV.).

A row of small stars is made across the board of every four strings, as described in previous pattern.

The upper half of a second star is worked across the board, underneath the others, and the strings are then cast on the next foundation cord.

Third row.—Foundation cord of macramé knots.

Fourth row.—Double diamond of eight strings, with filled centre of three double Genoese knots (Ex. XII.).

Fifth row.—Foundation cord of macramé knots.

Sixth row.—Insertion of two single stars, the same as described in row 3 of previous pattern.

Seventh row.—Foundation cord of macramé knots, and ends frayed as a fringe.

XXII. A FRINGE COMPOSED OF DIAMONDS AND GENOESE BARS.

This pattern combines exercises in Stages II and III. The boards must be strung with four foundation cords, and the strings cut 2 yards in length. Forty-eight strings are worked in every scallop, therefore twenty-four strings must be cast on to make a complete pattern. Five of these scallops make a handsome pattern for a bracket.

First row.—Cast on with plain macramé knots. Hold the string at the half and knot it on the cord just as all the foundation cords are worked and let both strings hang down of equal length.

Second row.—Take four strings, and tie two double chain knots (Ex. XLIII., Stage II.).

Third row.—Foundation cord of macramé knots.

Fourth row.—Single diamonds of eight strings with Genoese bar in centre.

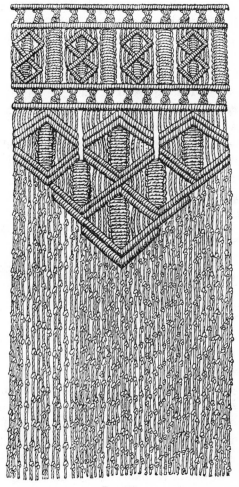

Fig. 127.

Follow the same directions for double diamond with filled centre (Ex. XII.), and carry the last leader across to the left and knot all seven strings upon it, and then work a second diamond immediately under the top one. The zig-zag bar is worked for each half of the diamond.

The next four strings are worked as a Genoese bar of the same length as the two diamonds. Take four strings, hold the second and third down and knot with the first and fourth (Ex. IX., Stage II.).

Fifth row.—Foundation cord of macramé knots.

Sixth row.—Same as second.   Two double chain knots.

Seventh row.—Foundation cord of macramé knots.

Scallop.—There are forty eight strings proceeding from the seventh foundation cord. These are divided into three, and sixteen strings taken for each large double diamond.

Let children count sixteen strings and put all others aside, so as not to get confused.

Take No. 8 string and No. 9 as leaders and slant them to the left and right over the other seven strings, each side to show design of pattern. Sketch on blackboard.

Let these two single bars be worked first, and then the second bar of each immediately under them, taking the two centre strings again for the two leaders. This completes the top half of diamond. Whilst this part is understood, let the children take the next two sets of sixteen strings and work the top halves of the next two diamonds.

Each diamond has a Genoese bar in the centre. Question how many strings are required for this bar. Where is the bar to be ?   In centre of diamond. Which strings must be taken for it ?   Seventh, eighth, ninth and tenth. Find these in each diamond.

Teacher should hastily inspect and see if the strings are

correctly picked out in each diamond and then allow the children to work their centre bars. When the knots are level with the lower corner of the top bars, then a half has been worked, and as many knots again must be done to meet the lower angle of diamond.

Finish diamonds and knot in the bars.

The adjoining sides of two diamonds form the upper half of another row of diamonds which are worked below.

Take two strings from the adjoining sides of the two upper diamonds and work a bar of Genoese knots with them, to form centre of new diamond.

Take the last leaders from the points of the preceding diamonds and slant them right and left, and knot two bars to form the lower half of diamond.

Two diamonds are made in this row to fit between the three above, and one in the third row which completes the scallop. Any one who has worked the exercises will be able to copy a pattern from an illustration better than from description. It will be noticed that as the same leader is continued across two diamonds, long beaded bars are made in the joining of the diamonds.

A long handsome fringe of single knots completes the pattern, which has involved the use of exercises in all three stages.

XXIII. SQUARES AND FAN SHAPES.

Preparation.—Macramé board strung with four foundation cords.

Strings 2 yards in length.

Ten picots or twenty working strings are required for each scallop.

First row.—Cast on two strings with double picot knot (Ex. v.).

Second row.—Chain bars of two knots with four strings.

Third row.—Foundation cord.

Fourth row.—Squares of macramé knots. Take ten strings for each square.

Take the *sixth* string as leader and hold it to the left across the first five, and knot each one twice upon it, beginning at the fifth string. Place each leader aside as it is used.

Next take the *seventh* string across as leader, and work the *same five* strings on it, and then leave that leader.

Take the eighth and ninth strings as leaders, and repeat until five bars are worked, and the lower corner of square comes exactly under the top corner.

All the leader threads hang to the left and the working strings to the right, and in this order they must be cast on the next foundation cord. It will be noticed that the five strings on the right act as five distinct leaders across the five strings on the left. They really cross each other in the pattern, and change places.

Fifth row.—Foundation cord.

Sixth row.—Same as second : chain bars of double knots.

Seventh row.—Foundation cord.

Eighth row.—This pattern may be termed " Fan Shapes," and children will see the likeness in that a fan graduates to a point, the same as in the pattern.

For the first " fan " take ten strings, and hold the tenth, ninth, eighth, seventh, sixth, fifth, fourth, and third as leaders over the others in succession, and as each leader is done with let it hang to the left, similar to the way the squares were worked.

Take another ten strings and work a corresponding fan to the right. Take first, second, third, fourth, fifth, sixth, seventh, and eighth strings in succession as leaders

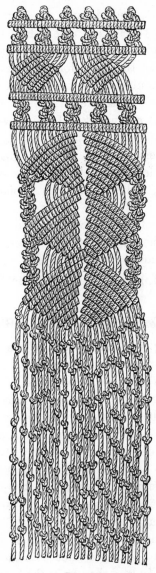

Fig. 128.

across the others, and do not touch the leaders when finished, but let them hang in order to the right.

Tie the fans together by the two central strings in one chain knot. Take the outer four strings of each fan and work a bar of double chain knots, eight in number.

Next take the two centre strings as leaders, right and left, and work two fans like those above, and hold the first leader of each fan slanting to meet the last knot of chain bar. When knotting on the strings of the chain bars to the first leader see that the four strings are taken in correct order, and that the knots come down close to the bar.

A third pair of fans is worked like the second, and the strings as they terminate as leaders are knotted in single knots to form a deep fringe.

This is a very pretty pattern for brackets.

XXIV. OPEN KNOTTING.

Open knotting is so called because the knots made are not tightened up close to the other work, but kept at regular distances apart with a space between.

Open knotting may be introduced almost in any part of a pattern. It is useful for filling up spaces, or for making a kind of network ground to a bold geometrical pattern, so as to define the outline more sharply.

The Solomon and Genoese flat knots are those most used for the exercise, and therefore it will be understood that *four* strings are always required for each knot.

First row.—Count the first four strings 1, 2, 3, 4. Fasten the two centre ones down and keep them straight in position, and make a Solomon's knot with the first and fourth (Ex. XXI., Stage II.), and then make the first half of the knot again. This is not necessary, but the Solomon's knot is more secure and looks better if three turns are made instead of two. A Genoese knot may be used instead.

Continue working a series of Solomon's knots with every four strings in a straight row across the board till all are used.

Second row.—Begin to work a second row of knots across the board.

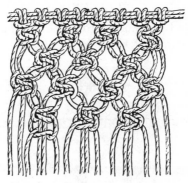

FIG. 129.

Leave the first two strands, and begin to count the sets of four from the third string. Therefore the second series of knots will consist of the third and fourth of one previous knot and the first and second of the next. Take this combination each time and hold the centre two strings down and knot with the first and fourth as before, making one and half turns for each knot. Work across the board till all are used.

Third row.—The knotting again begins with the first four strands, and so the pattern commences for every *uneven* number at the *beginning* of the row, and for every *even* number at the *third* string of every row.

The only difficulty to the children is regularity of the

knots and uniformity in the space between them. A little practice soon overcomes both these difficulties, but if the pattern is to be worked to any great depth, such as required for the foundation of a bag, then glass-headed pins should be used to hold the knot in position when tying, and so keep the pattern even.

XXV.   FRINGE OF BEADED BARS AND SINGLE DIAMONDS.

Prepare the frames or boards with four foundation cords, and cut the strings 1½ yards in length.

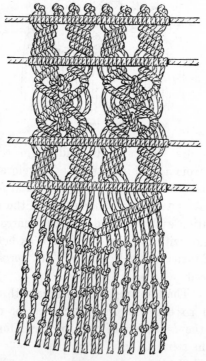

FIG. 130.

Heading.—Single knot picots, cast on first cord (Ex. IV.).

First pattern.—Beaded bars of four strings to the left and right (Ex. VII. and VIII.).

Foundation cord.—(Ex. III.).

Second pattern.—Two single diamonds worked with the same leaders throughout (Ex. XI. and XII.).

A double chain knot in centre of each, made with four strings, immediately top half of each diamond is knotted.

Foundation cord.—(Ex. III.).

Third pattern.—Beaded bars of four strings to the left and right (Ex. VII. and VIII.).

Foundation cord.—(Ex. III.).

Seventh pattern.—Two beaded bars of eight strings, worked right and left as top of a double star, and joined in the centre (Ex. XV.).

Fringe.—Each separate string knotted with single knots.

XXVI. CROSSBAR INSERTION.

This pattern, though illustrated here as an insertion, can be introduced into any fringe between two foundation cords. It is simply a variation of the beaded bars right and left, as taught in Exercises VII.-X. Eight strings are required for every group or double bar of knots, and therefore for the pattern the strings cast on must be a multiple of eight or divisible by eight.

Pattern.—*First row.*—Simple casting on with single strings.

Second row.—Foundation cord of macramé knots.

Third row.—Double beaded bars slanting to the left. Take eight strings and hold the eighth as leader, slanting across the seven to the left-hand corner of the board. Knot the seventh, sixth, fifth, fourth, third, second, and first upon it consecutively. Arrange the strings in order as they come from first bar, and again hold the right-hand string across the seven and knot a second bar close up to the last.

All the bars slanting to the left must be made straight across the board first, with every set of eight strings.

Fourth row.—Take every *fifth* string from each double bar as leader and hold to the right across seven strings. The seven strings will consist of three from the same bar and four from the next.

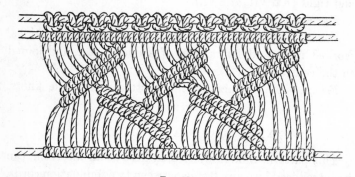

Fɪɢ. 131.

Begin the second series of bars slanting to the right, and make double beaded bars of eight strings in the same way as first set.

Fifth row.—Foundation cord of macramé knots.

The strings may be looped over another string to match the casting on and the pattern used as an insertion, or the ends may be used to continue another pattern, or fringed and knotted. Bags made of alternate strips of this insertion and open knotting (Ex. XXIV.) look very well together, or this insertion might be used as the heading of a bag, with the lower portion of open knotting. When a piece of work the depth required for a bag is finished, it is removed from the board, folded together, and the strings at the sides and bottom tied together.

XXVII.   BEADED BAR INSERTION.

This is a good supplementary pattern with which to start the quick children until the slower ones reach efficiency. Children who can work Exercises VII. to X. with any degree of accuracy should be allowed to work this pattern the entire length of their board, and the strings proceeding from the lower foundation cord may be used for another exercise, or be knotted and fringed.

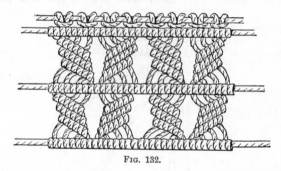

Fig. 132.

The pattern is the beaded bar of four strings worked three times right and left alternately, and then cast on a foundation cord.   This pattern also makes a good heading or insertion for hand-bags.

XXVIII.   TO FINISH OFF INSERTIONS.

Sometimes a band or strip is required without fringe, which is termed an insertion.   The pattern is always worked alike top and bottom.

To represent the "casting on" row at the bottom,

turn the work over and work a foundation cord on the *wrong* side; this will give the "casting on" appearance. Then take every two threads and tie together, and cut off strings close to the knot. Push the knot upwards on wrong side, or sew all down with needle and thread.

If a "picot" edge is to be represented, the strings must be knotted to match the heading, and the ends sewn down on the under side to the last foundation cord.

XXIX. JOINING ON A NEW STRING.

In working large patterns it will be found that some strings are much more used than others, and will require

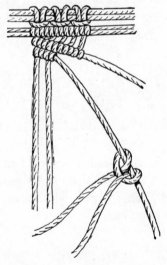

Fig. 133.

lengthening to finish the design in hand. When this is the case, a new strand may easily be added without trouble, and without any appearance of a join.

When a string is likely to become too short, arrange that it shall be lengthened, or rather replaced, when making a beaded bar, as this is the neatest way and best place for adding a new string.

Suppose the side of a star is being worked, and the third string is much shorter than the others, and, though long enough to finish the star, must be lengthened to finish the pattern.

Take the new string and turn down a few inches to form a loop. Thread the loop upon the leader string with the two unequal strands hanging down. Hold the upper one (the short end) in position with finger and thumb, and take the lower strand and bring across it and work half a macramé knot with it on the leader (Fig. 133). Push the string up into place and sew the short end to the underside of the work, and then cut off. This join will have the appearance of two beads, as in ordinary knotting, and the other strands of the star are then knotted on the leader in the usual way, and will keep the new one in place.

FRINGES FOR TOWELS AND MATS.

Some of the coarser kinds of linen towelling and canvas materials are suitable for making knotted fringes with the threads of the material. The cross threads must be drawn out, and the knotting threads unravelled about twice as long as the fringe is intended to be. If the material is too fine for the purpose, threads can be knotted on to the edge of the stuff, and a pattern worked with them to form a fringe.

Three simple illustrations are here given of how to knot on threads to the hem of mats and towels, etc.

Teachers will find that the honeycomb, cross-stitch, and other firm makes of canvas are useful in two ways, *e.g.* a class might take mats, doyleys, towels, tray cloths, children's feeders and pinafores, as an occupation in kindergarten sewing, and the knotting class could further add to the appearance of these articles by knotting on a fringe.

Whatever colours are used in the cross-stitch and darning patterns, the same should be used in the fringe.

XXX.   KNOTTING ON THREADS TO THE EDGE OF A MATERIAL.

1. Cut the strings double the length the fringe is to be, and fold them in half.

2. Take a steel crochet hook, suitable to the size of the thread, and push it through the edge of stuff, from wrong side to right. When the needle protrudes on the right side, catch hold of the loop of the doubled thread, and pull it through to the wrong side.

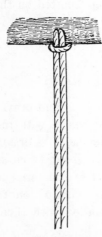

3. Put the ends which are on the right side down through the loop, and pull tight.

It will be noticed that the casting on is similar to that on a foundation cord, only in this case the material is the foundation.

Cast on as many strings as will be required for the pattern to be worked evenly.

Fig. 134.

Open knotting made of rows of knots, alternating in

each successive row, are most suitable for this purpose, because the patterns allow of being pulled into shape, and lie flat round the corners.

Three simple patterns composed of exercises in Stages I., II., and III. are here given, to show how the corners are managed.

The threads must always be added close together at the corners, or else additional strands must be added, as shown in turning corner of square mat (Fig. 138).

XXXI. A SINGLE TIE KNOT ON TWO STRINGS.

1. Cast on the strings about $\frac{1}{4}$ inch apart.

2. Take one string from each pair, and knot together with a single tie knot.

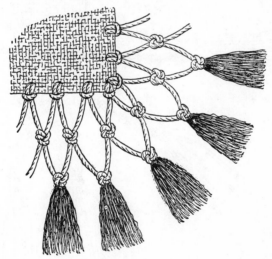

Fig. 135.

3. Separate knots, and take one string from each, and tie a second set of knots.

4. Fray ends as a tassel 1½ inches in length.

Note.—This pattern can be continued to any width, if strings are cut accordingly.

This pattern is worked in the hand, according to Ex. VI., Stage I.

XXXII. BARS OF SINGLE CHAIN KNOT.

1. Cast on strings about ¼ inch apart. Fix side of mat to board with drawing pins.

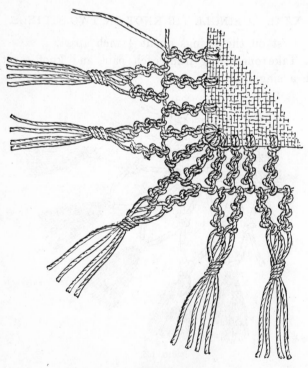

FIG. 136.

2. Tie six chain knots with every pair of strings.

3. Separate each pair, and tie six chain knots with one string from each preceding pair.

4. Take all strings together and tie a single tie knot to form a tassel.

XXXIII. SINGLE DIAMONDS WITH CROSSED CENTRES.

1. Cast on strings about $\frac{1}{8}$ inch apart.

2. Take four strings and work a beaded bar slanting to the left.

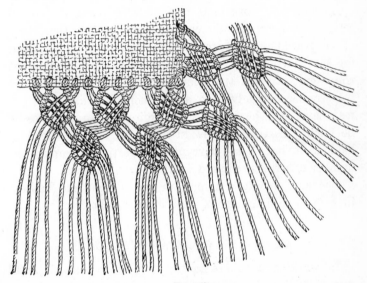

Fig. 137.

3. Take next four strings and work a beaded bar slanting to the right.

Note.—The strings now naturally cross in centre, therefore in completing the lower half of the diamond take the same leaders, but knot on them the strings coming from opposite side ; this will give the crossed appearance in centre.

4. Work a series of these diamonds all round the mat.

5. Work a second set of diamonds in same manner, but take *four* strings from right and left sides of two preceding diamonds with which to make the second set.

6. Knot all ends to form a fringe.

RULE FOR WORKING SQUARE AND ROUND MATS, AND ENLARGING A PATTERN.

As macramé work does not allow of being drawn up so as to turn corners, like crochet, netting, and other kinds of fancy needlework, supplementary strings must be added for that purpose. At an early stage of the enlargement these are cast on to a foundation cord, but when the pattern becomes advanced and of bold design, the strings may be added where necessity requires a gap or space to be filled. Casting on new strings must not be done at haphazard, but in strict regular proportion to supply the number of strings required for the next pattern.

The supplementary strings are pulled tight and knotted in with the others, until quite lost in the pattern.

XXXIV.   TO WORK A SQUARE MAT.

In working a square mat it is best to make a small square of open knotting for a beginning with Solomon knots, because into the loops all round of this pattern the new strands are easily added.

To begin, tie a foundation cord across the board and on it cast sixteen threads. With these work a perfect square of open knotting (Fig. 129).

Into each of the three sides cast on sixteen threads, to

correspond with the sixteen which were first cast on.
The first sixteen threads are worked to the bottom of the
open knotting, therefore sixteen threads must be added on
the foundation cord, one *between* each of those originally
cast on.

The beginning is now a square of open knotting, with
working threads proceeding out of each side.

Release the foundation cord from board, and pin the
square down at each corner with drawing pins.

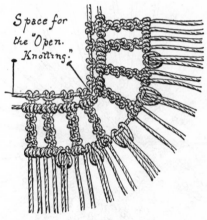

Space for
the "Open.
Knotting."

FIG. 138.

The cord is turned sharply down from the top and held
as a foundation cord, whilst each string is knotted twice on
it. It is carried round all three sides in this way, and then
knotted to its other end to make the square complete.
At each corner add two supplementary strings on the cord
to allow for turning easily. Keep the work fixed to the
board and measure accurately an exact square each time
a foundation cord is worked, and place tacks, etc., to keep
the work in position.

Any pattern may be worked after the cords, and the illustration (Fig. 138) shows how to add supplementary strings for the enlargement.

XXXV. TO WORK A ROUND KNOTTED MAT.

Materials required.—1. A brass ring 1½ inches in diameter.

2. Macramé strings, 2 yards in length.

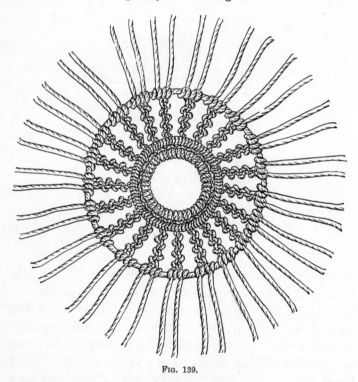

Fig. 139.

Method.—Double the strings in half and cast on in the ordinary way.

First round.—Pass the ends of string up through the ring and bring them over down through the loop. Twenty-eight strings are cast on the ring in this way.

Second round.—Hold a string or place a slightly larger ring over the strings as a foundation cord, and knot each string twice upon it. Keep the cord or ring close all round, and tie the two ends together when the round is finished, and push the knot underneath.

Third round.—Take every two strings consecutively and tie ten chain knots, *i.e.* five knots with each string. There will be twenty-eight bars round the circle.

Fourth round.—Here again a circular foundation cord has to be worked, and a proficient worker would easily manage to make a correct circle with a cord foundation, but for children it is best to provide them with a large ring the exact size, or make one of wire for the purpose. As this circle is larger more strings will have to be added to cover it, and these are cast on the foundation wire at regular distances of every fourth stitch round the circle. On completion of this foundation cord there should be eighty-eight strings.

Fifth round.—This round is composed of double stars (Ex. xv.). Take eight strings for each star and work eleven round the circle.

Sixth round.—The circle is still increasing in circumference, and will require more strings added. The new strings are looped on the sides of each star. The ends are passed up through the outer strings and brought over down through the loop. The pair from each star are tied together with two double chain knots.

Seventh round.—A circular foundation cord. Twenty-two strings were added to the stars in last round, and therefore

there will be 132 working strings proceeding from this
foundation cord.

Eighth round.—This round is also made of double stars of
greater size.   Take every set of twelve strings and make a
double star with raised Solomon's knot centre, as described

FIG. 140.

in Ex. XVI.   Cast on a string on each side of every star, and
knot with double chain knots as before.

Ninth round.—Circular foundation cord with 176 strings
proceeding from it.

Tenth round.—A fringe.   Take four strings and knot four

double chain knots. Cut off strings, leaving 1½ inches for fraying. Repeat for every four strings.

This mat measures 10 inches in diameter, and may be increased to any size by the addition of new strings at each successive round as described.

MACRAMÉ EXERCISES APPLIED TO USEFUL ARTICLES.

In a large class many of the children will work the exercises with such care that it is a great incentive to all if some of the pieces are applied to a use, and shown to the class. Many of the pieces are easily adapted to a use without much trouble, such as the making of wall-pockets, tidies, pincushions, handkerchief sachets, night-dress cases, hand-bags, etc. A few simple uses made from the exercises produced by all the class are here illustrated.

Cigar boxes, covered and lined and ornamented with macramé, make beautiful toilet pincushions, and toilet boxes to match are made of smaller pieces, as shown in Fig. 142.

Muff boxes cut in half, and covered and lined and then ornamented with macramé, make nice work boxes or fancy baskets, to which a handle of macramé mounted on card-board can be attached.

Light open fringes for trimming baskets, ends of window blinds, towels, scarves, etc., are all within the range of the children, and could be done by the quick workers in the fine twine or crochet cottons. For scarves, Berlin wool should be used, and loose knots chosen to allow for shrinking.

XXXVI. HANDKERCHIEF CASE.

Any square handkerchief case can have the flaps ornamented with four macramé corners, as shown in illustration.
In fact, the whole case could be knotted—first a square of
open knotting and then the four corners cast on and worked
from each side.

FIG. 141.

These dainty little articles look best in the fine macramé
corners are worked in this case and mounted on a plush
twine, which takes longer to do, therefore only four
square lined with quilted satin.

Pattern.—The pattern is simple, and easily managed by the children without help. It consists of a series of small stars worked row by row.

First row.—Cast on one foundation cord of the double twine, across the board.

Second row.—Take each string separately and tie a small knot on the end as a picot. Knot 104 strings with macramé knot to the foundation cord.

Third row.—Take four strings for each star, and work twenty-six small stars straight across the board.

Fourth row.—Leave two strings at the beginning and end of every successive row and lay aside, and start making the stars with the third and fourth and fifth and sixth strings. This narrows the work by *one* star every row until it comes to a point of one star.

There are twenty-six rows of stars worked, which should form just half a square in shape. The ends at the top, with single chain knots, are frayed out to form an edging. The two strings left at the beginning and end of each row of stars are similarly knotted and frayed out.

Four such pieces are worked for the corners of the handkerchief case, and the same shape might be used for the front of slipper watch-pockets.

XXXVII. TOILET BOX.

This useful article may be made of any of the patterns already given if worked to about 4 inches in depth. The foundation is a round cardboard box, made exactly the size of a pound jam-pot. Place the jar on the cardboard, pencil round the bottom, and cut out a circle for the bottom of box. Next measure round the jar, and cut a strip of

cardboard that length and depth. Fasten together with
small paper fasteners, and then sew to the circle for the

FIG. 142.

bottom. The children can prepare these cardboard foundations.

The macramé work looks much better if laid upon a contrasting colour or shade; therefore, before joining the cardboard portions together, cover both parts entirely in sateen and neatly oversew the edges. The top and bottom pieces are then easily sewn together. When the foundation is ready take the strip of macramé knotting and tie the foundation strings tightly together round the box, and finish neatly with needle and macramé thread of same colour. The jar can be placed inside for flowers or toilet use. Any round boxes sold at chemists containing powder may be decorated in this way and made into toilet boxes or pincushions, such as those shown in the illustration.

Pattern.—Prepare the board with four foundation cords. Cut strings 1½ yards in length of two colours—tan and blue strings.

Heading.—Button-hole looping (Ex. VI.). Cast on alternately one blue, then one tan, button-hole loop to measure 12 inches across the board.

First pattern.—Genoese bars of six stitches, three right and three left. There will be alternate bars of blue and tan.

Foundation cord.—(Ex. III.).

Second pattern.—Double diamond with filled centre of Genoese bars of six stitches right and left. Eight strings are taken for each half of the diamond (Ex. XII.).

When the first row of diamonds is complete, work a Genoese bar between each with the two outer strings of each diamond before beginning the lower cross bars. It will be noticed that this central pattern is simply a double zig-zag bar of three turns, using eight strings each time. Or it might be called a double diamond and a half. The Genoese bars are worked to form the centre of each diamond. The lower bars of top set of diamonds form the upper portion of the bottom set which are formed between the others, like in Ex. XXII.

Foundation cord.—(Ex. III.).

Third pattern.—Double star of eight strings (Ex. XV.).

Foundation cord.—(Ex. III.).

Fringe.—Each pair of strings is tied with four chain knots, and then frayed out.

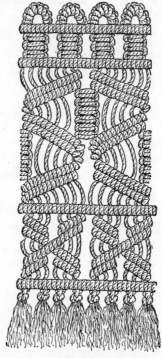

FIG. 143.

An inner lining of silk is gathered and sewn to the top of the foundation, and this lining is again hemmed and drawn up with a ribbon. In the illustration it is pulled up to show how made, but when in use should be pushed down, into the top of the box as a covering to its contents. The two coloured strings have a pretty effect in the knotting, and if the patterns be studied and the strings cast on accordingly, endless varieties and effects can be obtained by using two or more different coloured strings. A pretty ribbon is interlaced through the first row of bars and tied down from top to bottom with a full loop, to hide the knots which tie the pattern together.

XXXVIII. TOILET PINCUSHION.

Another easy and useful way of using up the small exercises produced in the class is to place them round

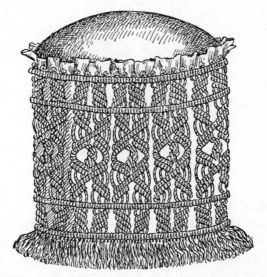

Fig. 144.

boxes, and utilize as work-boxes, pincushions, toilet-boxes, etc. Any small round boxes are suitable, or even square ones, but if the latter be used the pattern must be arranged to fill the sides, so that only the foundation cords turn the corners. The little box in illustration is a small cardboard powder box. The inside is first stuffed tightly with frayings and bran, and then over the whole is laid a thick layer of wool.

Two circles of blue velveteen, much larger than the top of box, are strained smoothly over the top and bottom of box, and kept in place by several windings of thread. A long strip of the material, with the edges turned in,

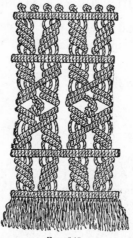

FIG. 145.

is gathered top and bottom, and caught to the circles which are tied over the top and bottom. The winding thread is hidden by the full sides, and the whole is made thoroughly neat before the piece of macramé is laid on.

Pattern.—Prepare the boards with four foundation strings, and cut *tan* brown working *threads* 1 yard in length. The fine macramé twine or thread No. 10 is used for this small article.

Cast on *forty* picots of single knotted strings (Ex. IV.).

First pattern.—Beaded bars of three rows, worked right and left upon four strings (Ex. VII. and VIII.).

Foundation cord of macramé knots (Ex. III.).

Centre pattern.—Two double stars, joined by a double chain knot.

Work a double star with first eight strings (Ex. XV.). When this star is complete, take the four strings which come from the exact centre, and knot the two from right half upon the two of the left, and reverse left upon right. Arrange strings in order and bring the same leaders across, and begin to work a second star. The first half of the second star will be the same as if completing a double diamond with filled centre (Ex. XII.).

Foundation cord.

Third pattern.—Beaded bars the same as first row.

XXXIX. WALL POCKET.

It will be noticed that the pattern of wall pocket is almost the same as the toilet pincushion. It is, in fact, a piece produced in the class when working the same exercise, and was just varied in the fringe to make it a little deeper for a pocket.

The pocket is 12 inches wide and 12 inches deep at the back, and about 6 inches deep in front. There is a side gusset on either side, to keep the front standing well out.

The cardboard shape is cut out, and each piece separately covered and oversewn, and then joined together before the macramé is added.

A narrow cord of single chain (Ex. XLI., Stage II.) is sewn on the extreme edge, and a flat cord of double chain (Ex. XLIII., Stage II.) is sewn on, about 1 inch from the edge, to ornament the back of the pocket.

The colour is heliotrope velveteen, and string to match.

The piece of macramé is 12 inches long and 6 inches

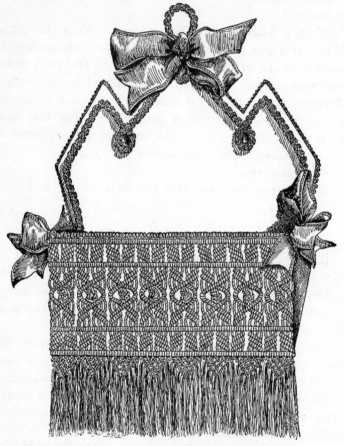

FIG. 146.

deep, and worked exactly as preceding pattern for toilet pincushion as far as the fringe.

Pattern.—1. Board strung with five foundation cords. Working strings cut 2 yards in length.

2. Cast on with single strings (Ex. I.).

3. Foundation cord of macramé knots (Ex. III.).

4. Beaded bars right and left of four strings (Ex. VII. and VIII.).

5. Two slanting bars right and left, single diamond with knotted centre, two slanting bars right and left.

6. Foundation cord of macramé knots (Ex. III.).

7. Beaded bars right and left of four strings (Ex. VII. and VIII.).

8. Foundation cord.

9. Fringe.—This is knotted to form small pointed scallops.

Take eight strings, and knot each pair together with chain knots.

Leave the first and last string of the eight, and tie chain knots on the three pairs left.

Again put aside the first and last string of the six just knotted, and tie knots on the four remaining.

Fig. 147.

Place first and last of the four aside, and knot together the one pair left. Cut all strings even, and fray out.

Treat every eight strings in the same way.

XL. SLIPPER WATCH-POCKET.

Exercises worked in the fine macramé twine No. 10, like the toilet pincushion and slipper watch-pocket, take longer to do, and therefore it is advisable only to make small articles in this fine twine, so that the children will

FIG. 148.

not tire of their pattern before it is finished. The same patterns worked in No. 4 string will produce a piece of work twice the size, which can be utilized for larger pockets or tidies.

These little slippers are made upon a foundation of two pieces of cardboard, both of which are covered in cheap crimson velveteen and lined at the back with sateen. The sole and the toe pieces are laid flat and covered on both sides with the material, and the edges neatly over-sewn in red silk or cotton all round. These pieces must be nicely tacked ready for the children to oversew.

If a good pattern be fixed with drawing pins to outline, the shapes might be pencilled and cut out by the children.

When the foundations are ready, the macramé is laid on and sewn in position.

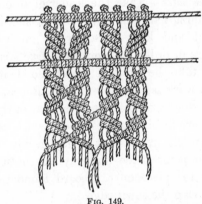

Fig. 149.

Pattern of toe of slipper.—The scallop is made up of a series of double stars, graduating, one less in each row, to terminate in a point. Prepare the board with two foundation cords of macramé twine of the same colour (tan No. 10). Cast on *twenty* single knotted picots (Ex. **IV.**), which will give *forty* working strings.

First pattern.—Beaded bars of three rows worked right and left upon every four strings (Ex. VII. and VIII.).

Foundation cord of macramé knots.

First row.—Work five double stars. Take every eight strings in succession for each star till the forty strings are used up (Ex. XV.).

Second row.—Arrange strings in order and work five more double stars with the same strings immediately under the first set. There are ten stars now worked, and the sides are straight.

Third row.—Work three perfect stars under the three centre ones of above row, but only work a half of the outside stars and leave four strings.

Fourth row.—One centre star and a half star on each side.

To finish the sides.—Take the leader of second bar when working the first half star and hold it slanting towards the toe point and knot *seven* strings on it. Stop and arrange strings in order. Count back *four* strings on this long bar, and take the *fourth* as leader and slant to point of toe again and work *seven* strings on it. Repeat.

Only the lower corner of star is omitted in the two rows, and the sides are finished as described, which can be easily copied from the diagram. Cut strings evenly about 1 inch long round the point of toe, and fray out the strings.

Mount the toe piece on cardboard foundation, and let the fringe overlap the sewn edge.

The sole part of slipper is decorated with a cord made of double chain bar (Ex. XLIII., Stage II.). Any of the cords in Stage II., if made in the fine twine, are very nice for ornamenting the edges of small needle-books, pincushions, tidies, etc. Two of these pockets are made and tied together as a pair of slippers, and a hook may be sewn on the heel portion on which to hang a watch and chain.

XLI. ROUND TOILET PINCUSHION.

The foundation of this pincushion is a round chocolate box about 6 inches in diameter. The inside is filled with frayings and bran as far as the rim, and then layers of wool are placed on the top. Over the top and bottom a circle of marone velveteen is stretched, the edge of which is kept secure by a tight winding of string round and round the side of the box. This plan is quicker and easier to manage than by sewing on the top and bottom, and the circle can be strained into position without creases, as these are arranged on the sides where the winding is done.

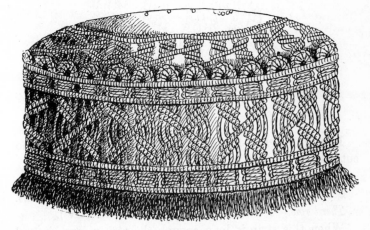

Fɪɢ. 150.

Now that the top and bottom of box are made neat, take a strip of velveteen to measure in width the depth of box, turn down the edges and tightly strain it round the side to cover the edges of circles. Let this band come close to the bottom and just to the rim of the box. Sew the ends neatly together, and the pincushion is ready for the macramé work.

Materials.—Macramé twine No. 10 in two colours, marone and green. The pieces used are exercises worked in the class and adapted to this purpose. There are two separate strips used for the decoration.

Top of pincushion.—This pattern is the simple one of double stars (Ex. XV.). One star and a half of another is worked each time.

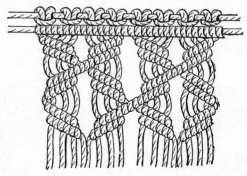

Fig. 151.

Top Pattern.—Fasten on two foundation cords, and cut strings 1 yard long.

First row.— Casting on according to simple method (Ex. I.).

Second row.—Foundation cord of macramé knots (Ex. III.).

Third row.—Double star and half a star (Ex. XV.).

When this strip is long enough the strings are knotted to a foundation cord, and sewn all round to the rim of the box. The ends of the foundation cords are joined, and the pattern drawn together with a tapestry needle and thread of same colour.

As the casting on was the simple method it allows of being drawn up, and this is done until the first cord tightens round the curve of the cushion and lies flat and regular. A few stitches here and there will keep it in position.

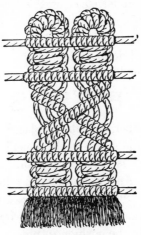

Fig. 152.

Side Pattern.—This comprises bars of the Genoese knot and a double star. The strip is about half a yard long and worked in two colours, marone and green strings.

Fasten on board four foundation cords, and cut strings 1½ yards in length.

1. Take two marone coloured strings, and work eight button-hole loops for picot and cast on (Ex. VI.). Repeat with two green strings. Alternate the picots along the entire length of board.

2. Foundation cord.—(Ex. III.).

3. Genoese bar of six stitches.

4. Foundation cord (Ex. III.).

5. Double star (Ex. XV.).

6. Same as No. 4.

7. Same as No. 3.

8. Same as No. 2. Cut ends and fringe.

This strip surrounds the box, and the picots are made to stand up above the rim. The first foundation cord is sewn to the one underneath of the first pattern, and the lowest foundation cord is sewn to the velveteen circle all round the bottom edge. The box looks extremely neat and well-finished if done as described.

As a finish, the letters

P I N S

are drawn on paper, which is placed upon the top of cushion, and a child lines in the pencil letters with small pins. The paper is torn away, and the word remains written in pins. Any style may be adopted, but if small squared paper be used, the letters can be drawn on the chequered kindergarten board and copied by child and then transferred to the cushion in pins.

EASY PATTERNS FOR DICTATION EXERCISES.

XLII. PATTERN 1.

1. Cast on twelve strings, simple casting on.
2. Work foundation cord.
3. Work six bars of Solomon's knots (ten stitches in each).
4. Foundation cord.
5. Work three double stars, with eight strings for each star.
6. Foundation cord.
7. Work six bars of Solomon's knots (ten stitches).
8. Foundation cord and knotted fringe.

XLIII. PATTERN 2.

1. Cast on twelve strings with single picots.
2. Button-hole bar to the right (four stitches).

3. Foundation cord.

4. A bannister bar (four strings), double star (sixteen strings), and bannister bar (four strings).

5. Foundation cord.

6. Button-hole bar to the left (four stitches).

7. Foundation cord and fringe.

XLIV. PATTERN 3.

1. Cast on twelve strings with double picots.

2. Six Genoese bars of eight knots (four strings).

3. Foundation cord.

4. Two double diamonds with filled centres (twelve strings for each diamond).

5. Foundation cord.

6. Six Genoese bars of eight knots.

7. Foundation cord.

8. Three single diamonds (eight strings to each), two worked below, and one to terminate in a point. Ends fringed.

XLV. PATTERN 4.

1. Cast on six button-hole picots of eight stitches.

2. Work a zig-zag bar of four turns, and a single star of eight strings, then another zig-zag bar, and so on.

3. Foundation cord.

4. Two treble stars with raised centres (twelve strings to each star).

5. Foundation cord.

6. Zig-zag bars and stars like second row.

7. Foundation cord.

8. Fringe of open knotting in Solomon's knots, to terminate in a point. Ends fringed.

XLVI. STRING RUGS.

This occupation is particularly suitable for the boys, because the work is rather firm and needs strong little fingers to hold a large piece. The work is made in strips, and then joined together afterwards. Door mats are quickly made in a class if the individual children be employed in knitting a strip for the centre or border.

Very durable hearthrugs for the bedroom or nursery can easily be made in the same way, and if the pattern be studied, may be made to look very effective and handsome.

Materials required.—1. A quantity of pieces or cuttings of cloth.

2. Balls of ordinary shop twine.

3. A pair of steel knitting needles, No. 10.

It is necessary to have a good store of cloth-cuttings before starting upon a large piece of work, so that the pattern can be carried out in its entirety. Tailors' old pattern cards and cuttings are very suitable, or any old cloth garments might have the best parts selected and used for the purpose. If possible, get some bright colours for the centre to intermix with the more sombre hues, and let the border consist of a strip of black or very dark cloth.

First, let the cloth be prepared, ready for use, and sorted, and the colours kept in separate boxes. The children will enjoy cutting the cloth into strips, which must be half an inch wide and 4 inches long, and both ends cut slanting. For the small door-mat, about to be described, red and black pieces of cloth are used. Old red army clothes are most useful for the work, because the bright colours contrast and brighten up the appearance of the whole.

Cast on about thirty stitches for each strip, this number will be found quite as many as a child can manage comfortably; and if the strip should be required wider, two narrow ones are easily sewn together, and may be worked quicker by two children than one wide strip. Knit the first row. In the second row knit the first stitch and then place one of the pieces of cloth across between the needles, knit another stitch and bring the end on the outside back across and between the needles, so that both ends are on the same side. Knit another stitch and place another piece of cloth and proceed as before. The children who are knitting the border strips will use all black or dark cloth, but those knitting the centre strips might use alternately one red and one dark piece of cloth. The centre of the door mat measures 24 inches long and 12 inches wide. As each knitted strip is about 4 inches wide it takes three strips 24 inches long, joined together to form the centre.

The border is also 4 inches wide, and is made by knitting two strips, 36 inches long, for the two long sides, and then filling in the ends with two strips, 12 inches long. In the accompanying diagram it will be seen how the strips are joined together. When the rug is finished the back or under side should be covered with a piece of coarse canvas.

Dark, 36 × 4.		
Dark, 12 × 4.	Red and Black, 24 × 4.	Dark, 12 × 4.
	Red and Black, 24 × 4.	
	Red and Black, 24 × 4.	
Dark, 36 × 4.		

HAIRPIN CROCHET WORK.

Hairpin Crochet Work is so called because it is worked on a kind of large hairpin or two-pronged fork. Large steel hairpins are made specially for this work, but for fine laces the ordinary japanned hairpin, of a coarse make, is quite suitable. The work is very easy to make, and is produced in strips of any length, which can be joined, and interlaced, and crocheted, in such a number of ways as to produce an unlimited variety of patterns.

The work has the appearance of a gimp with looped edges, and is worked with a crochet hook, in coloured crochet cottons or macramé string or twine.

When worked in the fine string, No. 10, the effect is most delicate, and very dainty things can be made of the work.

It is best to use *bone* crochet hooks and string, and the steel forks manufactured for the purpose, for children, so that no accident can happen in the use of the implements.

The forks are blunt at the points, and made of a stout wire that retains its shape, and are sold from 9d. to 2s. per dozen according to the size. The bone crochet hooks are sold at the same rate. The small outlay required for materials is one great recommendation of the occupation as a school subject, and also that the materials are lasting and need no renewal.

Very pretty laces, fringes, and edgings can be made in this work, and it can be intermingled with braid crochet with excellent effect.

It is not intended to deal deeply with the subject for children, and so only a few simple exercises are here given, which are quite within their range.

The suitability of the occupation for children is—

1. That the implements used are light and easily handled by a child without fear of accident.

2. That the outlay in apparatus required for a large class would be small compared with other occupations.

3. That the work can be undertaken by the whole class simultaneously.

4. That it is an attractive occupation to a child, because it increases rapidly and may be worked in colours.

5. That there is no waste of material, because for teaching purposes one length of string only need be used, which can easily be undone and used again, till perfection is obtained.

6. That the occupation is exceedingly simple, and readily learned by a child.

7. That the work goes on uninterruptedly to any length, without help from the teacher, and can be cut and fastened off without detriment to the appearance.

8. That the work is useful, and trains both hands to work equally.

The strips can be utilized in the following ways :

(*a*) Several strips can be joined together, either by a crochet chain, or by interlacing the loops, and be applied to the making of antimacassars, bedspreads, bags, cushion covers, short curtains, etc.

(*b*) The loops of short strips of six or eight inches in length can be drawn up tightly on one side to form rosettes, which may be crocheted or sewn together to form rounds or squares for doyleys, mats, toilet pincushion covers, nightdress cases, etc.

(*c*) A chain edge may be crocheted into the loops on one or both sides, to form edgings and insertions. If embroidery or coloured washing cottons are used, the work can be utilized for trimming household and body linen. The work looks very handsome, worked in macramé string No. 4, as curtain bands, box covers, bags, and antimacassars. For small articles the fine macramé twine No. 10 is best, and boxes and cushions covered in a contrasting shade look very nice with the work strained upon them.

Materials required.—1. A bone crochet hook the size of string used.

2. A steel hairpin or fork.

3. Macramé string or twine.

Method.—Common twine, or knitting cotton could be used for teaching purposes. Take crochet hook in right hand ; show how it is to be held. Explain the use of the hook, and how it always "dips under" the string on the left side to catch up a loop. Illustrate this with large hook before the class.

Let children take end of string, hold it between left finger and thumb, and strain remainder across the first, second, and third fingers, and then twist it once round the little finger as a kind of tension. The fingers must be wide apart for the needle to dip down. When this position is attained, let children work a chain until the crochet needle has lost its awkwardness, and the left hand is able to hold the string.

XLVII.   HAIRPIN CROCHET STITCH.

1. Make a single loop with crochet needle on the end of string.

2. Take crochet needle out of the loop, and insert downwards through it the left prong of the hairpin fork.

3. Hold the hairpin fork between the finger and thumb of the left hand, with points downwards, because the work

slips off as it increases without interruption; but if pre-
ferred the curved end can be held with the points upwards,
and if so, as soon as the fork is full, the stitches must be
slipped off and the last two threaded on again.

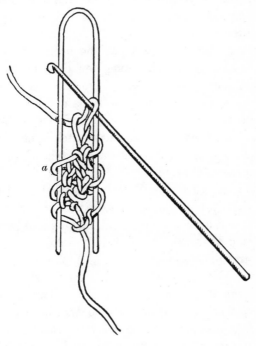

Fig. 153.

4. The thread must always be in front, next to the
worker, when a loop is to be made, therefore take the
thread across from left prong over the right, and across the
fingers of the left hand, as described for crochet chain.

5. Put the crochet needle into the loop on the left prong,
and pull up the thread across the fingers through it. Then
through this loop pull another, which is called "one chain."

This constitutes the "beginning" or "casting on," and there are now two loops on the fork—one on each prong.

The Stitch.—Keep the thread still across the fingers, and turn the fork over to the left; the thread will now be across the right prong, ready to take a loop. Put the crochet needle through the loop, and draw up the thread to make the new stitch on right prong, and then, *to tighten* each stitch after it is made, put the needle (with loop on it) into the stitch on left prong and draw up the thread. There are now two loops on the crochet needle; draw the thread up again through both loops at once. To those who understand crochet, this means work one double crochet into the left stitch after each new stitch is made on right. Turn fork, and repeat for every new stitch, which is always made on the *right* prong.

In the illustration (Fig. 153) the stitch has just been made on the right prong, and the needle will next go in the left loop at *a*, and draw up the thread, making two loops on the needle, and then the thread will be taken up again, and drawn through both loops at once. The thread must not pass round the left prong when taking up the thread through the left loop at *a*, it must be drawn up between the prongs.

Joining the Strips.—If the work be made in coarse macramé string, take *one* loop at a time for interlacing; but if the fine twine or crochet cottons are used, then take two or more loops each time.

Arrange two strips of same width and length end to end, and see that the last loop is finished off securely. That is simply done by pulling the end through the loop and drawing tight.

Take both strips at the end and hold in left hand, loop to loop. With crochet hook or fingers pull first loop of one strip through the first loop of second strip. Pull second loop of first strip through last loop, and then second loop of second strip through, and so interlace across each loop in succession to the bottom, when a stitch must be made, or the last loop tied to keep it from undoing.

Two loops drawn through two loops each time is very pretty, and also three loops drawn through three, but a crochet hook is needed for these triple loops, and each loop must be flat in position, and not get twisted in the interlacing. Another way of joining is by crocheting the strips together with a long chain of crochet.

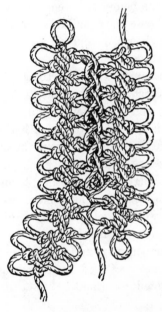

FIG. 154.

Scallops and rosettes are formed in drawing up several loops on one side tightly, and then joining together with a chain of crochet. It is very fascinating to children to crochet, and a chain is simple and easy to do, and will help in another occupation—"Crochet over moulds and rings."

CROCHET WITH COLOURED THREAD AND MOULDS.

Any child who can crochet the simple stitches (chain and double crochet) described in "Hairpin Work," can take up this occupation without any further teaching. The moulds are made in stiff cardboard of various shapes, and sold from one penny to threepence per dozen according to the size. Those most suitable for children are circles and hearts which are devoid of sharp angles too difficult for a child to turn nicely.

The fine macramé twine No. 10 is used for this work, also coloured crochet cotton, silks, and linen threads, all of which look well for different purposes.

Large moulds should be used with the macramé twine, and small with the silks and linen threads.

The moulds are simply covered in double crochet stitches; they may have another fancy edge added in chain stitch if desired. The centres are always filled in with a spider web of gold thread, or of the same thread that was used for the mould.

When a number of moulds have been worked by the children they are arranged to form patterns, and then sewn or crocheted together.

XLVII. TO CROCHET MOULDS FOR HANDKERCHIEF CASE AND GLOVE CASE.

Materials required.—1. A fine bone crochet hook.

2. A cardboard circle the size of a halfpenny.

3. A ball of macramé twine.

Method.—There must be a stitch on the needle to begin with.

1. Make a loop at the end of string.

2. Hold the mould between finger and thumb of the left hand, with curved surface upwards.

3. Place string across fingers of left hand as in all crochet work.

4. With loop on needle, put needle through the centre of circle and draw up the thread, making two loops on the needle; pull these into position at the edge of the ring, and take up the thread again and draw through both stitches at once.

It will be noticed that each loop drawn up covers the circle with two threads each time, and gives a chain edge at the rim.

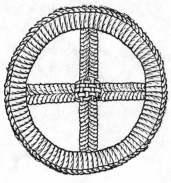

FIG. 155.

5. The centres of the moulds are darned across. Two long threads are crossed over the centre of circle and re-crossed at right angles. A long needleful of thread is joined on and woven to and fro across the two strings, as seen in illustration. If liked, a gold thread made to imitate a wheel or spider's web can be worked instead.

XLIX. HANDKERCHIEF AND GLOVE CASES.

These pretty articles are made of crochet covered moulds as described above.   They are about the size of a penny, and crocheted in flax thread, which has the glossy appear-

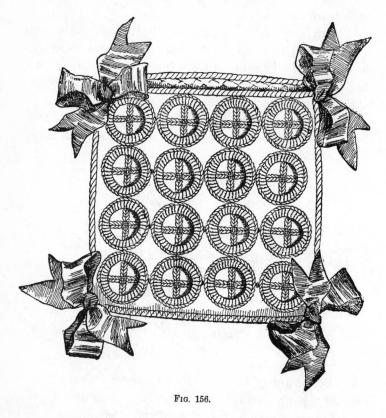

Fig. 156.

ance of silk and is less expensive.   The thread is bought in skeins at 3¾d per dozen in any colour, and is strong, and will wash and wear well.   The moulds are worked

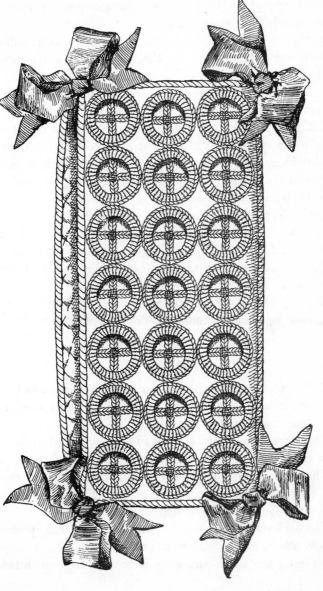

Fig. 157.

in flax thread of apple green, and mounted upon rose
pink sateen as a good contrast.

Sufficient rings might be worked to cover both sides,
but in the illustration only the top side is ornamented
with the moulds.

About half a yard of quilted satin in green or rose
colour is sufficient to cut both articles.

After joining the moulds together to the size required,
double the quilted satin and cut a little larger. Cover
the wadding side with the sateen, and finish with a cord
all round the edge. Then mount and sew on the moulds,
and finish each corner with a bow of green ribbon.

Each case is first made like a book cover, a double
square of 6 inches for the handkerchief case, and an
oblong 12 inches by 6 for the glove case.

The moulds may be used on both sides and no lining
used at all.

Bags, pockets, tidies, brackets, mantel borders, mats,
etc., may be made of these crocheted moulds.

L. WALL POCKET.

This wall pocket is made upon stout wire, which is
first nicely shaped and then entirely crocheted over in
the same manner as the moulds.

There are two separate parts to the pocket, which however correspond in size in the lower portion.

The pocket portion measures 6 inches across at top,
and narrows to $1\frac{1}{2}$ inches at the bottom (Fig. 159). Here
the wires overlap and are tied securely together.

The back portion is shaped exactly like the front pocket
except at the top, where it is curved in to form a loop.
In shaping the back portion it is best to begin with this

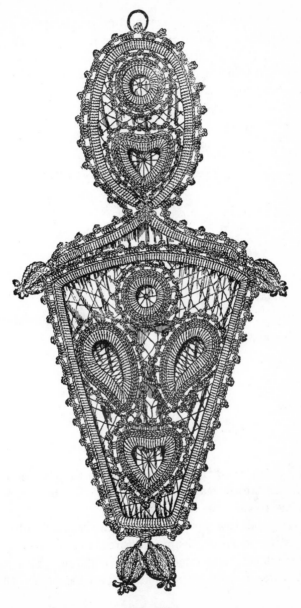

Fig. 158.

loop, and take the middle portion of the piece of wire and shape it upon a round object, then tie the wires together and spread them out till 6 inches across for the pocket portion (Fig. 160). Bend the wires upon a corner of a box to get a good even turn, and then measure the back to correspond with the front portion.

The front pocket is 8 inches deep, and the back portion $13\frac{1}{2}$ inches from top to bottom.

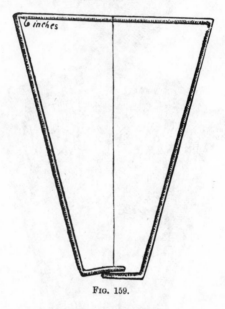

6 inches

Fig. 159.

Having shaped the wire foundations they are crocheted over in brown macramé twine No. 10, beginning and ending at the join of the wire.

A second row of crochet is again worked all round, consisting of three chain and three double crochet, both of which are understood by the children. This second round is crocheted in salmon pink twine.

The foundation wires may be covered in Stage II. knotting with as good effect. The back and front portions are now interlaced across corner-ways with strands of thread, like the "Gridiron Wall-Pocket" and "Tennis Racquet," and are then ready for the moulds.

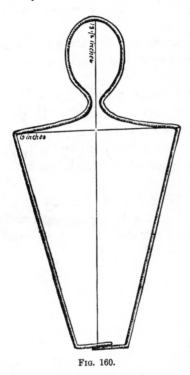

FIG. 160.

Three different shapes, heart, circle, and pine, are used in the decoration of pocket. Two of each shape are crocheted over to match the wire foundation, and then arranged on the interlaced strings and sewn in position at the back.

A lining of thin yellow silk or sateen is gathered full

and placed over each part to show between the interlacings, and sewn neatly to the wire foundation all round.

Both parts are now complete and ready for joining together.

First, join the lower edge of back and front portions together by oversewing with needle and twine of same colour.

Pull the front portion forward about 4 or 6 inches, and fill in the sides with a gusset of gathered yellow Surah silk.

Draw up the lower portion tightly and sew in at the bottom, and at the upper edge of the gusset turn down a deep hem and make a heading, so that an elastic run through draws up a little frill at the top. By having an elastic as the running string the pocket can be opened to a greater width.

Four little balls, worked over like the " Tennis Ball," are sewn on, one at each corner and two at the bottom. A small ring is sewn at the top by which to suspend the pocket.

A CATALOGUE OF SELECTED DOVER BOOKS
IN ALL FIELDS OF INTEREST

A CATALOGUE OF SELECTED DOVER BOOKS
IN ALL FIELDS OF INTEREST

AMERICA'S OLD MASTERS, James T. Flexner. Four men emerged unexpectedly from provincial 18th century America to leadership in European art: Benjamin West, J. S. Copley, C. R. Peale, Gilbert Stuart. Brilliant coverage of lives and contributions. Revised, 1967 edition. 69 plates. 365pp. of text.

21806-6 Paperbound $3.00

FIRST FLOWERS OF OUR WILDERNESS: AMERICAN PAINTING, THE COLONIAL PERIOD, James T. Flexner. Painters, and regional painting traditions from earliest Colonial times up to the emergence of Copley, West and Peale Sr., Foster, Gustavus Hesselius, Feke, John Smibert and many anonymous painters in the primitive manner. Engaging presentation, with 162 illustrations. xxii + 368pp.

22180-6 Paperbound $3.50

THE LIGHT OF DISTANT SKIES: AMERICAN PAINTING, 1760-1835, James T. Flexner. The great generation of early American painters goes to Europe to learn and to teach: West, Copley, Gilbert Stuart and others. Allston, Trumbull, Morse; also contemporary American painters—primitives, derivatives, academics—who remained in America. 102 illustrations. xiii + 306pp.

22179-2 Paperbound $3.00

A HISTORY OF THE RISE AND PROGRESS OF THE ARTS OF DESIGN IN THE UNITED STATES, William Dunlap. Much the richest mine of information on early American painters, sculptors, architects, engravers, miniaturists, etc. The only source of information for scores of artists, the major primary source for many others. Unabridged reprint of rare original 1834 edition, with new introduction by James T. Flexner, and 394 new illustrations. Edited by Rita Weiss. 6⅝ x 9⅝.

21695-0, 21696-9, 21697-7 Three volumes, Paperbound $13.50

EPOCHS OF CHINESE AND JAPANESE ART, Ernest F. Fenollosa. From primitive Chinese art to the 20th century, thorough history, explanation of every important art period and form, including Japanese woodcuts; main stress on China and Japan, but Tibet, Korea also included. Still unexcelled for its detailed, rich coverage of cultural background, aesthetic elements, diffusion studies, particularly of the historical period. 2nd, 1913 edition. 242 illustrations. lii + 439pp. of text.

20364-6, 20365-4 Two volumes, Paperbound $6.00

THE GENTLE ART OF MAKING ENEMIES, James A. M. Whistler. Greatest wit of his day deflates Oscar Wilde, Ruskin, Swinburne; strikes back at inane critics, exhibitions, art journalism; aesthetics of impressionist revolution in most striking form. Highly readable classic by great painter. Reproduction of edition designed by Whistler. Introduction by Alfred Werner. xxxvi + 334pp.

21875-9 Paperbound $2.50

PLANETS, STARS AND GALAXIES: DESCRIPTIVE ASTRONOMY FOR BEGINNERS, A. E. Fanning. Comprehensive introductory survey of astronomy: the sun, solar system, stars, galaxies, universe, cosmology; up-to-date, including quasars, radio stars, etc. Preface by Prof. Donald Menzel. 24pp. of photographs. 189pp. 5¼ x 8¼.
21680-2 Paperbound $1.50

TEACH YOURSELF CALCULUS, P. Abbott. With a good background in algebra and trig, you can teach yourself calculus with this book. Simple, straightforward introduction to functions of all kinds, integration, differentiation, series, etc. "Students who are beginning to study calculus method will derive great help from this book." Faraday House Journal. 308pp. 20683-1 Clothbound $2.00

TEACH YOURSELF TRIGONOMETRY, P. Abbott. Geometrical foundations, indices and logarithms, ratios, angles, circular measure, etc. are presented in this sound, easy-to-use text. Excellent for the beginner or as a brush up, this text carries the student through the solution of triangles. 204pp. 20682-3 Clothbound $2.00

TEACH YOURSELF ANATOMY, David LeVay. Accurate, inclusive, profusely illustrated account of structure, skeleton, abdomen, muscles, nervous system, glands, brain, reproductive organs, evolution. "Quite the best and most readable account,' Medical Officer. 12 color plates. 164 figures. 311pp. 4¾ x 7.
21651-9 Clothbound $2.50

TEACH YOURSELF PHYSIOLOGY, David LeVay. Anatomical, biochemical bases; digestive, nervous, endocrine systems; metabolism; respiration; muscle; excretion; temperature control; reproduction. "Good elementary exposition," The Lancet. 6 color plates. 44 illustrations. 208pp. 4¼ x 7. 21658-6 Clothbound $2.50

THE FRIENDLY STARS, Martha Evans Martin. Classic has taught naked-eye observation of stars, planets to hundreds of thousands, still not surpassed for charm, lucidity, adequacy. Completely updated by Professor Donald H. Menzel, Harvard Observatory. 25 illustrations. 16 x 30 chart. x + 147pp. 21099-5 Paperbound $1.25

MUSIC OF THE SPHERES: THE MATERIAL UNIVERSE FROM ATOM TO QUASAR, SIMPLY EXPLAINED, Guy Murchie. Extremely broad, brilliantly written popular account begins with the solar system and reaches to dividing line between matter and nonmatter; latest understandings presented with exceptional clarity. Volume One: Planets, stars, galaxies, cosmology, geology, celestial mechanics, latest astronomical discoveries; Volume Two: Matter, atoms, waves, radiation, relativity, chemical action, heat, nuclear energy, quantum theory, music, light, color, probability, antimatter, antigravity, and similar topics. 319 figures. 1967 (second) edition. Total of xx + 644pp. 21809-0, 21810-4 Two volumes, Paperbound $5.00

OLD-TIME SCHOOLS AND SCHOOL BOOKS, Clifton Johnson. Illustrations and rhymes from early primers, abundant quotations from early textbooks, many anecdotes of school life enliven this study of elementary schools from Puritans to middle 19th century. Introduction by Carl Withers. 234 illustrations. xxxiii + 381pp.
21031-6 Paperbound $2.50

THE ARCHITECTURE OF COUNTRY HOUSES, Andrew J. Downing. Together with Vaux's *Villas and Cottages* this is the basic book for Hudson River Gothic architecture of the middle Victorian period. Full, sound discussions of general aspects of housing, architecture, style, decoration, furnishing, together with scores of detailed house plans, illustrations of specific buildings, accompanied by full text. Perhaps the most influential single American architectural book. 1850 edition. Introduction by J. Stewart Johnson. 321 figures, 34 architectural designs. xvi + 560pp.
22003-6 Paperbound $4.00

LOST EXAMPLES OF COLONIAL ARCHITECTURE, John Mead Howells. Full-page photographs of buildings that have disappeared or been so altered as to be denatured, including many designed by major early American architects. 245 plates. xvii + 248pp. 7⅞ x 10¾.
21143-6 Paperbound $3.50

DOMESTIC ARCHITECTURE OF THE AMERICAN COLONIES AND OF THE EARLY REPUBLIC, Fiske Kimball. Foremost architect and restorer of Williamsburg and Monticello covers nearly 200 homes between 1620-1825. Architectural details, construction, style features, special fixtures, floor plans, etc. Generally considered finest work in its area. 219 illustrations of houses, doorways, windows, capital mantels. xx + 314pp. 7⅞ x 10¾.
21743-4 Paperbound $4.00

EARLY AMERICAN ROOMS: 1650-1858, edited by Russell Hawes Kettell. Tour of 12 rooms, each representative of a different era in American history and each furnished, decorated, designed and occupied in the style of the era. 72 plans and elevations, 8-page color section, etc., show fabrics, wall papers, arrangements, etc. Full descriptive text. xvii + 200pp. of text. 8⅜ x 11¼.
21633-0 Paperbound $5.00

THE FITZWILLIAM VIRGINAL BOOK, edited by J. Fuller Maitland and W. B. Squire. Full modern printing of famous early 17th-century ms. volume of 300 works by Morley, Byrd, Bull, Gibbons, etc. For piano or other modern keyboard instrument; easy to read format. xxxvi + 938pp. 8⅜ x 11.
21068-5, 21069-3 Two volumes, Paperbound $10.00

KEYBOARD MUSIC, Johann Sebastian Bach. Bach Gesellschaft edition. A rich selection of Bach's masterpieces for the harpsichord: the six English Suites, six French Suites, the six Partitas (Clavierübung part I), the Goldberg Variations (Clavierübung part IV), the fifteen Two-Part Inventions and the fifteen Three-Part Sinfonias. Clearly reproduced on large sheets with ample margins; eminently playable. vi + 312pp. 8⅛ x 11.
22360-4 Paperbound $5.00

THE MUSIC OF BACH: AN INTRODUCTION, Charles Sanford Terry. A fine, nontechnical introduction to Bach's music, both instrumental and vocal. Covers organ music, chamber music, passion music, other types. Analyzes themes, developments, innovations. x + 114pp.
21075-8 Paperbound $1.25

BEETHOVEN AND HIS NINE SYMPHONIES, Sir George Grove. Noted British musicologist provides best history, analysis, commentary on symphonies. Very thorough, rigorously accurate; necessary to both advanced student and amateur music lover. 436 musical passages. vii + 407 pp.
20334-4 Paperbound $2.75

JOHANN SEBASTIAN BACH, Philipp Spitta. One of the great classics of musicology, this definitive analysis of Bach's music (and life) has never been surpassed. Lucid, nontechnical analyses of hundreds of pieces (30 pages devoted to St. Matthew Passion, 26 to B Minor Mass). Also includes major analysis of 18th-century music. 450 musical examples. 40-page musical supplement. Total of xx + 1799pp.

(EUK) 22278-0, 22279-9 Two volumes, Clothbound $15.00

MOZART AND HIS PIANO CONCERTOS, Cuthbert Girdlestone. The only full-length study of an important area of Mozart's creativity. Provides detailed analyses of all 23 concertos, traces inspirational sources. 417 musical examples. Second edition. 509pp.   (USO) 21271-8 Paperbound $3.50

THE PERFECT WAGNERITE: A COMMENTARY ON THE NIBLUNG'S RING, George Bernard Shaw. Brilliant and still relevant criticism in remarkable essays on Wagner's Ring cycle, Shaw's ideas on political and social ideology behind the plots, role of Leitmotifs, vocal requisites, etc. Prefaces. xxi + 136pp.

21707-8 Paperbound $1.50

DON GIOVANNI, W. A. Mozart. Complete libretto, modern English translation; biographies of composer and librettist; accounts of early performances and critical reaction. Lavishly illustrated. All the material you need to understand and appreciate this great work. Dover Opera Guide and Libretto Series; translated and introduced by Ellen Bleiler. 92 illustrations. 209pp.

21134-7 Paperbound $1.50

HIGH FIDELITY SYSTEMS: A LAYMAN'S GUIDE, Roy F. Allison. All the basic information you need for setting up your own audio system: high fidelity and stereo record players, tape records, F.M. Connections, adjusting tone arm, cartridge, checking needle alignment, positioning speakers, phasing speakers, adjusting hums, trouble-shooting, maintenance, and similar topics. Enlarged 1965 edition. More than 50 charts, diagrams, photos. iv + 91pp.   21514-8 Paperbound $1.25

REPRODUCTION OF SOUND, Edgar Villchur. Thorough coverage for laymen of high fidelity systems, reproducing systems in general, needles, amplifiers, preamps, loudspeakers, feedback, explaining physical background. "A rare talent for making technicalities vividly comprehensible," R. Darrell, High Fidelity. 69 figures. iv + 92pp.   21515-6 Paperbound $1.00

HEAR ME TALKIN' TO YA: THE STORY OF JAZZ AS TOLD BY THE MEN WHO MADE IT, Nat Shapiro and Nat Hentoff. Louis Armstrong, Fats Waller, Jo Jones, Clarence Williams, Billy Holiday, Duke Ellington, Jelly Roll Morton and dozens of other jazz greats tell how it was in Chicago's South Side, New Orleans, depression Harlem and the modern West Coast as jazz was born and grew. xvi + 429pp.

21726-4 Paperbound $2.50

FABLES OF AESOP, translated by Sir Roger L'Estrange. A reproduction of the very rare 1931 Paris edition; a selection of the most interesting fables, together with 50 imaginative drawings by Alexander Calder. v + 128pp. 6½x9¼.

21780-9 Paperbound $1.25

POEMS OF ANNE BRADSTREET, edited with an introduction by Robert Hutchinson. A new selection of poems by America's first poet and perhaps the first significant woman poet in the English language. 48 poems display her development in works of considerable variety—love poems, domestic poems, religious meditations, formal elegies, "quaternions," etc. Notes, bibliography. viii + 222pp.

22160-1 Paperbound $2.00

THREE GOTHIC NOVELS: THE CASTLE OF OTRANTO BY HORACE WALPOLE; VATHEK BY WILLIAM BECKFORD; THE VAMPYRE BY JOHN POLIDORI, WITH FRAGMENT OF A NOVEL BY LORD BYRON, edited by E. F. Bleiler. The first Gothic novel, by Walpole; the finest Oriental tale in English, by Beckford; powerful Romantic supernatural story in versions by Polidori and Byron. All extremely important in history of literature; all still exciting, packed with supernatural thrills, ghosts, haunted castles, magic, etc. xl + 291pp.

21232-7 Paperbound $2.50

THE BEST TALES OF HOFFMANN, E. T. A. Hoffmann. 10 of Hoffmann's most important stories, in modern re-editings of standard translations: Nutcracker and the King of Mice, Signor Formica, Automata, The Sandman, Rath Krespel, The Golden Flowerpot, Master Martin the Cooper, The Mines of Falun, The King's Betrothed, A New Year's Eve Adventure. 7 illustrations by Hoffmann. Edited by E. F. Bleiler. xxxix + 419pp. 21793-0 Paperbound $3.00

GHOST AND HORROR STORIES OF AMBROSE BIERCE, Ambrose Bierce. 23 strikingly modern stories of the horrors latent in the human mind: The Eyes of the Panther, The Damned Thing, An Occurrence at Owl Creek Bridge, An Inhabitant of Carcosa, etc., plus the dream-essay, Visions of the Night. Edited by E. F. Bleiler. xxii + 199pp. 20767-6 Paperbound $1.50

BEST GHOST STORIES OF J. S. LEFANU, J. Sheridan LeFanu. Finest stories by Victorian master often considered greatest supernatural writer of all. Carmilla, Green Tea, The Haunted Baronet, The Familiar, and 12 others. Most never before available in the U. S. A. Edited by E. F. Bleiler. 8 illustrations from Victorian publications. xvii + 467pp. 20415-4 Paperbound $3.00

MATHEMATICAL FOUNDATIONS OF INFORMATION THEORY, A. I. Khinchin. Comprehensive introduction to work of Shannon, McMillan, Feinstein and Khinchin, placing these investigations on a rigorous mathematical basis. Covers entropy concept in probability theory, uniqueness theorem, Shannon's inequality, ergodic sources, the E property, martingale concept, noise, Feinstein's fundamental lemma, Shanon's first and second theorems. Translated by R. A. Silverman and M. D. Friedman. iii + 120pp. 60434-9 Paperbound $1.75

SEVEN SCIENCE FICTION NOVELS, H. G. Wells. The standard collection of the great novels. Complete, unabridged. *First Men in the Moon, Island of Dr. Moreau, War of the Worlds, Food of the Gods, Invisible Man, Time Machine, In the Days of the Comet.* Not only science fiction fans, but every educated person owes it to himself to read these novels. 1015pp. 20264-X Clothbound $5.00

AGAINST THE GRAIN (A REBOURS), Joris K. Huysmans. Filled with weird images, evidences of a bizarre imagination, exotic experiments with hallucinatory drugs, rich tastes and smells and the diversions of its sybarite hero Duc Jean des Esseintes, this classic novel pushed 19th-century literary decadence to its limits. Full unabridged edition. Do not confuse this with abridged editions generally sold. Introduction by Havelock Ellis. xlix + 206pp. 22190-3 Paperbound $2.00

VARIORUM SHAKESPEARE: HAMLET. Edited by Horace H. Furness; a landmark of American scholarship. Exhaustive footnotes and appendices treat all doubtful words and phrases, as well as suggested critical emendations throughout the play's history. First volume contains editor's own text, collated with all Quartos and Folios. Second volume contains full first Quarto, translations of Shakespeare's sources (Belleforest, and Saxo Grammaticus), Der Bestrafte Brudermord, and many essays on critical and historical points of interest by major authorities of past and present. Includes details of staging and costuming over the years. By far the best edition available for serious students of Shakespeare. Total of xx + 905pp.
21004-9, 21005-7, 2 volumes, Paperbound $7.00

A LIFE OF WILLIAM SHAKESPEARE, Sir Sidney Lee. This is the standard life of Shakespeare, summarizing everything known about Shakespeare and his plays. Incredibly rich in material, broad in coverage, clear and judicious, it has served thousands as the best introduction to Shakespeare. 1931 edition. 9 plates. xxix + 792pp. (USO) 21967-4 Paperbound $3.75

MASTERS OF THE DRAMA, John Gassner. Most comprehensive history of the drama in print, covering every tradition from Greeks to modern Europe and America, including India, Far East, etc. Covers more than 800 dramatists, 2000 plays, with biographical material, plot summaries, theatre history, criticism, etc. "Best of its kind in English," New Republic. 77 illustrations. xxii + 890pp.
20100-7 Clothbound $8.50

THE EVOLUTION OF THE ENGLISH LANGUAGE, George McKnight. The growth of English, from the 14th century to the present. Unusual, non-technical account presents basic information in very interesting form: sound shifts, change in grammar and syntax, vocabulary growth, similar topics. Abundantly illustrated with quotations. Formerly Modern English in the Making. xii + 590pp.
21932-1 Paperbound $3.50

AN ETYMOLOGICAL DICTIONARY OF MODERN ENGLISH, Ernest Weekley. Fullest, richest work of its sort, by foremost British lexicographer. Detailed word histories, including many colloquial and archaic words; extensive quotations. Do not confuse this with the Concise Etymological Dictionary, which is much abridged. Total of xxvii + 830pp. 6½ x 9¼.
21873-2, 21874-0 Two volumes, Paperbound $6.00

FLATLAND: A ROMANCE OF MANY DIMENSIONS, E. A. Abbott. Classic of science-fiction explores ramifications of life in a two-dimensional world, and what happens when a three-dimensional being intrudes. Amusing reading, but also useful as introduction to thought about hyperspace. Introduction by Banesh Hoffmann. 16 illustrations. xx + 103pp. 20001-9 Paperbound $1.00

INCIDENTS OF TRAVEL IN YUCATAN, John L. Stephens. Classic (1843) exploration of jungles of Yucatan, looking for evidences of Maya civilization. Stephens found many ruins; comments on travel adventures, Mexican and Indian culture. 127 striking illustrations by F. Catherwood. Total of 669 pp.
20926-1, 20927-X Two volumes, Paperbound $5.00

INCIDENTS OF TRAVEL IN CENTRAL AMERICA, CHIAPAS, AND YUCATAN, John L. Stephens. An exciting travel journal and an important classic of archeology. Narrative relates his almost single-handed discovery of the Mayan culture, and exploration of the ruined cities of Copan, Palenque, Utatlan and others; the monuments they dug from the earth, the temples buried in the jungle, the customs of poverty-stricken Indians living a stone's throw from the ruined palaces. 115 drawings by F. Catherwood. Portrait of Stephens. xii + 812pp.
22404-X, 22405-8 Two volumes, Paperbound $6.00

A NEW VOYAGE ROUND THE WORLD, William Dampier. Late 17-century naturalist joined the pirates of the Spanish Main to gather information; remarkably vivid account of buccaneers, pirates; detailed, accurate account of botany, zoology, ethnography of lands visited. Probably the most important early English voyage, enormous implications for British exploration, trade, colonial policy. Also most interesting reading. Argonaut edition, introduction by Sir Albert Gray. New introduction by Percy Adams. 6 plates, 7 illustrations. xlvii + 376pp. 6½ x 9¼.
21900-3 Paperbound $3.00

INTERNATIONAL AIRLINE PHRASE BOOK IN SIX LANGUAGES, Joseph W. Bátor. Important phrases and sentences in English paralleled with French, German, Portuguese, Italian, Spanish equivalents, covering all possible airport-travel situations; created for airline personnel as well as tourist by Language Chief, Pan American Airlines. xiv + 204pp.
22017-6 Paperbound $2.00

STAGE COACH AND TAVERN DAYS, Alice Morse Earle. Detailed, lively account of the early days of taverns; their uses and importance in the social, political and military life; furnishings and decorations; locations; food and drink; tavern signs, etc. Second half covers every aspect of early travel; the roads, coaches, drivers, etc. Nostalgic, charming, packed with fascinating material. 157 illustrations, mostly photographs. xiv + 449pp.
22518-6 Paperbound $4.00

NORSE DISCOVERIES AND EXPLORATIONS IN NORTH AMERICA, Hjalmar R. Holand. The perplexing Kensington Stone, found in Minnesota at the end of the 19th century. Is it a record of a Scandinavian expedition to North America in the 14th century? Or is it one of the most successful hoaxes in history. A scientific detective investigation. Formerly *Westward from Vinland*. 31 photographs, 17 figures. x + 354pp.
22014-1 Paperbound $2.75

A BOOK OF OLD MAPS, compiled and edited by Emerson D. Fite and Archibald Freeman. 74 old maps offer an unusual survey of the discovery, settlement and growth of America down to the close of the Revolutionary war: maps showing Norse settlements in Greenland, the explorations of Columbus, Verrazano, Cabot, Champlain, Joliet, Drake, Hudson, etc., campaigns of Revolutionary war battles, and much more. Each map is accompanied by a brief historical essay. xvi + 299pp. 11 x 13¾.
22084-2 Paperbound $6.00

A HISTORY OF COSTUME, Carl Köhler. Definitive history, based on surviving pieces of clothing primarily, and paintings, statues, etc. secondarily. Highly readable text, supplemented by 594 illustrations of costumes of the ancient Mediterranean peoples, Greece and Rome, the Teutonic prehistoric period; costumes of the Middle Ages, Renaissance, Baroque, 18th and 19th centuries. Clear, measured patterns are provided for many clothing articles. Approach is practical throughout. Enlarged by Emma von Sichart. 464pp.   21030-8 Paperbound $3.50

ORIENTAL RUGS, ANTIQUE AND MODERN, Walter A. Hawley. A complete and authoritative treatise on the Oriental rug—where they are made, by whom and how, designs and symbols, characteristics in detail of the six major groups, how to distinguish them and how to buy them. Detailed technical data is provided on periods, weaves, warps, wefts, textures, sides, ends and knots, although no technical background is required for an understanding. 11 color plates, 80 halftones, 4 maps. vi + 320pp. 6⅛ x 9⅛.   22366-3 Paperbound $5.00

TEN BOOKS ON ARCHITECTURE, Vitruvius. By any standards the most important book on architecture ever written. Early Roman discussion of aesthetics of building, construction methods, orders, sites, and every other aspect of architecture has inspired, instructed architecture for about 2,000 years. Stands behind Palladio, Michelangelo, Bramante, Wren, countless others. Definitive Morris H. Morgan translation. 68 illustrations. xii + 331pp.   20645-9 Paperbound $3.50

THE FOUR BOOKS OF ARCHITECTURE, Andrea Palladio. Translated into every major Western European language in the two centuries following its publication in 1570, this has been one of the most influential books in the history of architecture. Complete reprint of the 1738 Isaac Ware edition. New introduction by Adolf Placzek, Columbia Univ. 216 plates. xxii + 110pp. of text. 9½ x 12¾.
        21308-0 Clothbound $10.00

STICKS AND STONES: A STUDY OF AMERICAN ARCHITECTURE AND CIVILIZATION, Lewis Mumford.One of the great classics of American cultural history. American architecture from the medieval-inspired earliest forms to the early 20th century; evolution of structure and style, and reciprocal influences on environment. 21 photographic illustrations. 238pp.   20202-X Paperbound $2.00

THE AMERICAN BUILDER'S COMPANION, Asher Benjamin. The most widely used early 19th century architectural style and source book, for colonial up into Greek Revival periods. Extensive development of geometry of carpentering, construction of sashes, frames, doors, stairs; plans and elevations of domestic and other buildings. Hundreds of thousands of houses were built according to this book, now invaluable to historians, architects, restorers, etc. 1827 edition. 59 plates. 114pp. 7⅞ x 10¾.
        22236-5 Paperbound $3.50

DUTCH HOUSES IN THE HUDSON VALLEY BEFORE 1776, Helen Wilkinson Reynolds. The standard survey of the Dutch colonial house and outbuildings, with constructional features, decoration, and local history associated with individual homesteads. Introduction by Franklin D. Roosevelt. Map. 150 illustrations. 469pp. 6⅝ x 9¼.   21469-9 Paperbound $4.00

JIM WHITEWOLF: THE LIFE OF A KIOWA APACHE INDIAN, Charles S. Brant, editor. Spans transition between native life and acculturation period, 1880 on. Kiowa culture, personal life pattern, religion and the supernatural, the Ghost Dance, breakdown in the White Man's world, similar material. 1 map. xii + 144pp.
22015-X Paperbound $1.75

THE NATIVE TRIBES OF CENTRAL AUSTRALIA, Baldwin Spencer and F. J. Gillen. Basic book in anthropology, devoted to full coverage of the Arunta and Warramunga tribes; the source for knowledge about kinship systems, material and social culture, religion, etc. Still unsurpassed. 121 photographs, 89 drawings. xviii + 669pp.
21775-2 Paperbound $5.00

MALAY MAGIC, Walter W. Skeat. Classic (1900); still the definitive work on the folklore and popular religion of the Malay peninsula. Describes marriage rites, birth spirits and ceremonies, medicine, dances, games, war and weapons, etc. Extensive quotes from original sources, many magic charms translated into English. 35 illustrations. Preface by Charles Otto Blagden. xxiv + 685pp.
21760-4 Paperbound $4.00

HEAVENS ON EARTH: UTOPIAN COMMUNITIES IN AMERICA, 1680-1880, Mark Holloway. The finest nontechnical account of American utopias, from the early Woman in the Wilderness, Ephrata, Rappites to the enormous mid 19th-century efflorescence; Shakers, New Harmony, Equity Stores, Fourier's Phalanxes, Oneida, Amana, Fruitlands, etc. "Entertaining and very instructive." *Times Literary Supplement.* 15 illustrations. 246pp.
21593-8 Paperbound $2.00

LONDON LABOUR AND THE LONDON POOR, Henry Mayhew. Earliest (c. 1850) sociological study in English, describing myriad subcultures of London poor. Particularly remarkable for the thousands of pages of direct testimony taken from the lips of London prostitutes, thieves, beggars, street sellers, chimney-sweepers, street-musicians, "mudlarks," "pure-finders," rag-gatherers, "running-patterers," dock laborers, cab-men, and hundreds of others, quoted directly in this massive work. An extraordinarily vital picture of London emerges. 110 illustrations. Total of lxxvi + 1951pp. 6⅝ x 10.
21934-8, 21935-6, 21936-4, 21937-2 Four volumes, Paperbound $14.00

HISTORY OF THE LATER ROMAN EMPIRE, J. B. Bury. Eloquent, detailed reconstruction of Western and Byzantine Roman Empire by a major historian, from the death of Theodosius I (395 A.D.) to the death of Justinian (565). Extensive quotations from contemporary sources; full coverage of important Roman and foreign figures of the time. xxxiv + 965pp. 21829-5 Record, book, album. Monaural. $3.50

AN INTELLECTUAL AND CULTURAL HISTORY OF THE WESTERN WORLD, Harry Elmer Barnes. Monumental study, tracing the development of the accomplishments that make up human culture. Every aspect of man's achievement surveyed from its origins in the Paleolithic to the present day (1964); social structures, ideas, economic systems, art, literature, technology, mathematics, the sciences, medicine, religion, jurisprudence, etc. Evaluations of the contributions of scores of great men. 1964 edition, revised and edited by scholars in the many fields represented. Total of xxix + 1381pp. 21275-0, 21276-9, 21277-7 Three volumes, Paperbound $7.75

THE PHILOSOPHY OF THE UPANISHADS, Paul Deussen. Clear, detailed statement of upanishadic system of thought, generally considered among best available. History of these works, full exposition of system emergent from them, parallel concepts in the West. Translated by A. S. Geden. xiv + 429pp.
21616-0 Paperbound $3.00

LANGUAGE, TRUTH AND LOGIC, Alfred J. Ayer. Famous, remarkably clear introduction to the Vienna and Cambridge schools of Logical Positivism; function of philosophy, elimination of metaphysical thought, nature of analysis, similar topics. "Wish I had written it myself," Bertrand Russell. 2nd, 1946 edition. 160pp.
20010-8 Paperbound $1.35

THE GUIDE FOR THE PERPLEXED, Moses Maimonides. Great classic of medieval Judaism, major attempt to reconcile revealed religion (Pentateuch, commentaries) and Aristotelian philosophy. Enormously important in all Western thought. Unabridged Friedländer translation. 50-page introduction. lix + 414pp.
(USO) 20351-4 Paperbound $2.50

OCCULT AND SUPERNATURAL PHENOMENA, D. H. Rawcliffe. Full, serious study of the most persistent delusions of mankind: crystal gazing, mediumistic trance, stigmata, lycanthropy, fire walking, dowsing, telepathy, ghosts, ESP, etc., and their relation to common forms of abnormal psychology. Formerly *Illusions and Delusions of the Supernatural and the Occult.* iii + 551pp. 20503-7 Paperbound $3.50

THE EGYPTIAN BOOK OF THE DEAD: THE PAPYRUS OF ANI, E. A. Wallis Budge. Full hieroglyphic text, interlinear transliteration of sounds, word for word translation, then smooth, connected translation; Theban recension. Basic work in Ancient Egyptian civilization; now even more significant than ever for historical importance, dilation of consciousness, etc. clvi + 377pp. 6½ x 9¼.
21866-X Paperbound $3.95

PSYCHOLOGY OF MUSIC, Carl E. Seashore. Basic, thorough survey of everything known about psychology of music up to 1940's; essential reading for psychologists, musicologists. Physical acoustics; auditory apparatus; relationship of physical sound to perceived sound; role of the mind in sorting, altering, suppressing, creating sound sensations; musical learning, testing for ability, absolute pitch, other topics. Records of Caruso, Menuhin analyzed. 88 figures. xix + 408pp.
21851-1 Paperbound $2.75

THE I CHING (THE BOOK OF CHANGES), translated by James Legge. Complete translated text plus appendices by Confucius, of perhaps the most penetrating divination book ever compiled. Indispensable to all study of early Oriental civilizations. 3 plates. xxiii + 448pp. 21062-6 Paperbound $3.00

THE UPANISHADS, translated by Max Müller. Twelve classical upanishads: Chandogya, Kena, Aitareya, Kaushitaki, Isa, Katha, Mundaka, Taittiriyaka, Brhadaranyaka, Svetasvatara, Prasna, Maitriyana. 160-page introduction, analysis by Prof. Müller. Total of 826pp. 20398-0, 20399-9 Two volumes, Paperbound $5.00

DESIGN BY ACCIDENT; A BOOK OF "ACCIDENTAL EFFECTS" FOR ARTISTS AND DESIGNERS, James F. O'Brien. Create your own unique, striking, imaginative effects by "controlled accident" interaction of materials: paints and lacquers, oil and water based paints, splatter, crackling materials, shatter, similar items. Everything you do will be different; first book on this limitless art, so useful to both fine artist and commercial artist. Full instructions. 192 plates showing "accidents," 8 in color. viii + 215pp. 8⅜ x 11¼. 21942-9 Paperbound $3.50

THE BOOK OF SIGNS, Rudolf Koch. Famed German type designer draws 493 beautiful symbols: religious, mystical, alchemical, imperial, property marks, runes, etc. Remarkable fusion of traditional and modern. Good for suggestions of timelessness, smartness, modernity. Text. vi + 104pp. 6⅛ x 9¼. 20162-7 Paperbound $1.25

HISTORY OF INDIAN AND INDONESIAN ART, Ananda K. Coomaraswamy. An unabridged republication of one of the finest books by a great scholar in Eastern art. Rich in descriptive material, history, social backgrounds; Sunga reliefs, Rajput paintings, Gupta temples, Burmese frescoes, textiles, jewelry, sculpture, etc. 400 photos. viii + 423pp. 6⅜ x 9¾. 21436-2 Paperbound $4.00

PRIMITIVE ART, Franz Boas. America's foremost anthropologist surveys textiles, ceramics, woodcarving, basketry, metalwork, etc.; patterns, technology, creation of symbols, style origins. All areas of world, but very full on Northwest Coast Indians. More than 350 illustrations of baskets, boxes, totem poles, weapons, etc. 378 pp. 20025-6 Paperbound $3.00

THE GENTLEMAN AND CABINET MAKER'S DIRECTOR, Thomas Chippendale. Full reprint (third edition, 1762) of most influential furniture book of all time, by master cabinetmaker. 200 plates, illustrating chairs, sofas, mirrors, tables, cabinets, plus 24 photographs of surviving pieces. Biographical introduction by N. Bienenstock. vi + 249pp. 9⅞ x 12¾. 21601-2 Paperbound $4.00

AMERICAN ANTIQUE FURNITURE, Edgar G. Miller, Jr. The basic coverage of all American furniture before 1840. Individual chapters cover type of furniture— clocks, tables, sideboards, etc.—chronologically, with inexhaustible wealth of data. More than 2100 photographs, all identified, commented on. Essential to all early American collectors. Introduction by H. E. Keyes. vi + 1106pp. 7⅞ x 10¾. 21599-7, 21600-4 Two volumes, Paperbound $11.00

PENNSYLVANIA DUTCH AMERICAN FOLK ART, Henry J. Kauffman. 279 photos, 28 drawings of tulipware, Fraktur script, painted tinware, toys, flowered furniture, quilts, samplers, hex signs, house interiors, etc. Full descriptive text. Excellent for tourist, rewarding for designer, collector. Map. 146pp. 7⅞ x 10¾. 21205-X Paperbound $2.50

EARLY NEW ENGLAND GRAVESTONE RUBBINGS, Edmund V. Gillon, Jr. 43 photographs, 226 carefully reproduced rubbings show heavily symbolic, sometimes macabre early gravestones, up to early 19th century. Remarkable early American primitive art, occasionally strikingly beautiful; always powerful. Text. xxvi + 207pp. 8⅜ x 11¼. 21380-3 Paperbound $3.50

MATHEMATICAL PUZZLES FOR BEGINNERS AND ENTHUSIASTS, Geoffrey Mott-Smith. 189 puzzles from easy to difficult—involving arithmetic, logic, algebra, properties of digits, probability, etc.—for enjoyment and mental stimulus. Explanation of mathematical principles behind the puzzles. 135 illustrations. viii + 248pp.
20198-8 Paperbound $1.75

PAPER FOLDING FOR BEGINNERS, William D. Murray and Francis J. Rigney. Easiest book on the market, clearest instructions on making interesting, beautiful origami. Sail boats, cups, roosters, frogs that move legs, bonbon boxes, standing birds, etc. 40 projects; more than 275 diagrams and photographs. 94pp.
20713-7 Paperbound $1.00

TRICKS AND GAMES ON THE POOL TABLE, Fred Herrmann. 79 tricks and games—some solitaires, some for two or more players, some competitive games—to entertain you between formal games. Mystifying shots and throws, unusual caroms, tricks involving such props as cork, coins, a hat, etc. Formerly *Fun on the Pool Table*. 77 figures. 95pp.
21814-7 Paperbound $1.00

HAND SHADOWS TO BE THROWN UPON THE WALL: A SERIES OF NOVEL AND AMUSING FIGURES FORMED BY THE HAND, Henry Bursill. Delightful picturebook from great-grandfather's day shows how to make 18 different hand shadows: a bird that flies, duck that quacks, dog that wags his tail, camel, goose, deer, boy, turtle, etc. Only book of its sort. vi + 33pp. 6½ x 9¼. 21779-5 Paperbound $1.00

WHITTLING AND WOODCARVING, E. J. Tangerman. 18th printing of best book on market. "If you can cut a potato you can carve" toys and puzzles, chains, chessmen, caricatures, masks, frames, woodcut blocks, surface patterns, much more. Information on tools, woods, techniques. Also goes into serious wood sculpture from Middle Ages to present, East and West. 464 photos, figures. x + 293pp.
20965-2 Paperbound $2.00

HISTORY OF PHILOSOPHY, Julián Marías. Possibly the clearest, most easily followed, best planned, most useful one-volume history of philosophy on the market; neither skimpy nor overfull. Full details on system of every major philosopher and dozens of less important thinkers from pre-Socratics up to Existentialism and later. Strong on many European figures usually omitted. Has gone through dozens of editions in Europe. 1966 edition, translated by Stanley Appelbaum and Clarence Strowbridge. xviii + 505pp.
21739-6 Paperbound $3.00

YOGA: A SCIENTIFIC EVALUATION, Kovoor T. Behanan. Scientific but non-technical study of physiological results of yoga exercises; done under auspices of Yale U. Relations to Indian thought, to psychoanalysis, etc. 16 photos. xxiii + 270pp.
20505-3 Paperbound $2.50

Prices subject to change without notice.
Available at your book dealer or write for free catalogue to Dept. GI, Dover Publications, Inc., 180 Varick St., N. Y., N. Y. 10014. Dover publishes more than 150 books each year on science, elementary and advanced mathematics, biology, music, art, literary history, social sciences and other areas.